The Information and Knowledge Professional's Career Handbook

CHANDOS
INFORMATION PROFESSIONAL SERIES

Series Editor: Ruth Rikowski
(email: Rikowskigr@aol.com)

Chandos' new series of books is aimed at the busy information professional. They have been specially commissioned to provide the reader with an authoritative view of current thinking. They are designed to provide easy-to-read and (most importantly) practical coverage of topics that are of interest to librarians and other information professionals. If you would like a full listing of current and forthcoming titles, please visit our website www.chandospublishing.com or email info@chandospublishing.com or telephone +44 (0) 1223 891358.

New authors: we are always pleased to receive ideas for new titles; if you would like to write a book for Chandos, please contact Dr Glyn Jones on email gjones@chandospublishing.com or telephone number +44 (0) 1993 848726.

Bulk orders: some organisations buy a number of copies of our books. If you are interested in doing this, we would be pleased to discuss a discount. Please email info@ chandospublishing.com or telephone +44 (0) 1223 891358.

The Information and Knowledge Professional's Career Handbook

Define and create your success

ULLA DE STRICKER

AND

JILL HURST-WAHL

CP

CHANDOS
PUBLISHING

Oxford Cambridge New Delhi

Chandos Publishing
TBAC Business Centre
Avenue 4
Station Lane
Witney
Oxford OX28 4BN
UK
Tel: +44 (0) 1993 848726
Email: info@chandospublishing.com
www.chandospublishing.com

Chandos Publishing is an imprint of Woodhead Publishing Limited

Woodhead Publishing Limited
80 High Street
Sawston, Cambridge CB22 3HJ
UK
Tel: +44 (0) 1223 499140
Fax: +44 (0) 1223 832819
www.woodheadpublishing.com

First published in 2011

ISBN:
978 1 84334 608 1

British Library Cataloguing-in-Publication Data.
A catalogue record for this book is available from the British Library.

Typeset by Domex e-Data Pvt. Ltd.
Printed in the UK and USA.

Contents

1   **Introduction: an invitation**   **1**

     Overview: what is in this book   3

2   **An opaque profession: special challenges**   **7**

     Some professions are universally understood   8

     What do people know about what we do?   9

     Fashioning the value message   10

     Implications: getting used to promotional activities   13

     Show us the money: what money?   15

     You mean... I have to sell myself constantly?   16

     The good news: selling value by giving value   17

3   **Knowing who you are: your 'work personality' and your 'best fit'**   **19**

     Work preferences are personal   22

     Our fundamental approach to work vs. personal life   24

     Questions to ponder   26

     Implications for types of environments   27

     Your natural role   31

     Developing your personal skills: a growth plan   33

     What can you do? Plenty!   35

4   **Developing your brand: the professional image**   **41**

     Do you know how others see you?   42

     The core of our brand: the value we offer, the difference we make   44

Choosing a brand: rely on natural strengths 45

Supporting a brand: reputation and visibility
in traditional and new media 46

Professional associations: key to brand building 47

Professional demeanor: it's all about confidence 50

Professional polish: appearance matters 55

Tattoos, piercings, and purple hair: proceed
with deliberation! 65

5   **Looking for a job: tips and tricks** **69**

Going on a hunt 69

Conventional and unconventional hunting locations 70

Using bait to attract big game 74

Big game sighted! 75

Surviving the interview call 77

Who pays for the hunting road trip? 79

Hunters look for tracks (or what do your feet say?) 80

Big game crossing 80

We've been there 81

6   **Creating your story: crafting a compelling resume** **85**

Print vs. online 86

Resume as sales instrument 86

Three common myths: don't believe them! 87

Essential sections in a resume 89

Accuracy, consistency, and economy of words 95

Visual appearance 96

The cover letter 102

7   **Knowing where you want to go: plan... but let**
chance have a chance! **105**

Getting ready for the trip 106

Taking a detour... or two 107

Watch out for rough roads ahead – but use them
to your advantage   108

Arriving at your destination   111

8   Navigating organizational culture: understanding politics   115

Become familiar with the organizational structure
and culture   115

Gain political power   117

Understand the words   118

Create a common bond   119

Deal with abuse   120

Deal with conflict   121

A few dos, don'ts, and watch-outs   122

9   Winning support: 'selling' proposals with the
business case approach   127

But don't good ideas sell themselves?   128

What is the business case approach?   130

If money isn't involved – what about grassroots
support for an idea or initiative?   137

How are credibility and social capital built?   138

What does grassroots persuasion 'look like'?   139

The 'business case in reverse': demonstrating
existing value   142

The testimonial evidence   143

The ROI calculation   144

10 Making the leap to a managerial role: being the boss   149

A management role is not a must   150

What is the definition of 'manager'?   150

What does a manager 'do'?   151

Typical management challenges   153

How can one learn to become a (better) manager?
There has to be a way!   154

What you need: basic skills 156

What you need: personal abilities 159

A unique challenge: being promoted from a team to manage it 160

Reap the rewards 161

11 Resilience at work: coping when things get tough   163

It's tough all over – let's pull together 163

An attitude of gratitude 164

A positive atmosphere is everyone's responsibility 166

Dealing with difficult people 167

'But I hate my work' 168

Should you quit? 169

The bottom line: trust your gut 170

12 About the money   173

What are you worth? 173

What is in a compensation package? 174

What is in a benefits package? 176

When benefits are more important than money 178

How to assess a job offer and negotiate your compensation 178

The salary roller coaster 180

Trade or labor unions 181

Other professional organizations 182

In the end, it's not about the money 183

Measuring your success 184

13 Passing it on: collegial support or mentoring   185

Passing on knowledge and skills to others 185

What is meant by mentoring? 186

Where do you start? Just go ahead! 192

The unmentorables 196

14 Our colleagues speak: career snapshots   **201**

    Constance Ard   201

    Lori Bell   206

    Patrick Danowski   208

    Eli Edwards   211

    Nicole Engard   215

    Sergio Felter   219

    Stacey Greenwell   222

    Michael C. Habib   225

    Bruce Harpham   229

    Ruth Kneale   230

    Jane Kinney Meyers   234

    Alison Miller   238

    Pauline Nicholas   242

    Karolien Selhorst   245

    Bente Lund Weisbjerg   247

    Questions our colleagues want to ask   250

15 Jill and Ulla speak: our professional journeys   **253**

    Jill's story   253

    Ulla's story   261

Epilogue   **275**

Resources   **277**

Index   **279**

Introduction: an invitation

Dear Reader,

We have prepared our career book for our current and future colleagues in all the professions associated with information, knowledge, and learning:

- librarians or curators working in libraries, museums, archives, and similar entities focusing on collecting, protecting, and making accessible various objects through such functions as digitization, indexing, and web display

- those in academic settings who identify, organize, and make available to faculty and students the content and tools they need

- researchers supporting news media, publishers, and entities related to arts and culture

- those in specialized roles supporting the management, protection, and accessibility of records, data, information, and knowledge in all kinds of organizations in all sectors

- those holding information technology roles, working on intranets or websites or with social media

- those in the information industries who support publishers, aggregators, search engine and software providers, and similar players

- copyright, patent, and digital rights specialists managing ownership and access to content
- independents who operate research businesses or consultancies.

Whether you are an experienced or a brand new professional, are considering entering a graduate program leading to a Master's degree (variously named – MIS, MI, MLS are common), or are contemplating furthering your previous education with specialized certifications in, say, records management, we speak to you.

We invite you to think about your professional life in new ways, see your opportunities in new contexts, and plan now – no matter how new or advanced you may be in your career – for the next steps. So please deface the pages with your own thoughts, festoon the book with sticky notes, and be in touch with us!

In our work roles, we have had many opportunities to engage with our colleagues in discussion about the choices we make daily as well as at life-changing junctures. Looking back and around us as our profession is changing fast, we collected the key topics and arranged them in brief chapters, each intended to raise questions only you can answer for yourself. Our distillation of experience – in some cases direct, in other cases informed by the thought, 'now that we look back, perhaps another option deserved more weight' – is presented for you to consult as each topic becomes relevant for you. Although sequenced with a logical progression in mind, each chapter stands alone. Our topics reflect what we each 'wish we'd known before we learned it the hard way' as well as inspiration from watching our colleagues at work and at professional events over the years. Feel free to start where you like.

Why this book?

When you chose a profession that isn't instantly and universally recognized for its work and value (the way, say, veterinarians' and engineers' professions are), you set yourself up for a fair amount of future work some professionals don't typically have to do – justifying your value and making the case why you should be hired or your department's budget sustained or increased. We would like to help you minimize that work so as to maximize the time you have available for demonstrating your value to remove all doubt.

Your graduate school education prepared you for a range of technical and professional undertakings... but it may not have emphasized the social and interpersonal skills you need to get along with colleagues, build relationships, create a brand for yourself, and give that brand professional visibility. You may feel unprepared to take on managerial or project management roles or to resolve conflict in the workplace, and you may wonder what is the best way to lead meetings and encourage team members and staff to do their best work. In short, you may feel very confident in your technical skills yet anything but confident in your social and interpersonal ones.

That's why we wanted to share our experience. As the saying goes, we have 'been there, done that', and feel we have 'seen it all'. At times it was deeply painful, at times exhilarating – but we learned a lot, and we'd like to pass our lessons on by commenting on topics you may not encounter at the professional conferences you attend. We trust you will understand that we are blunt and honest about some things that may be awkward to discuss – and we hope our messages may save you headaches and speed your path to success!

Overview: what is in the book

In Chapter 2, we comment on a unique characteristic of the profession you have chosen and the ensuing need you may experience – throughout your career – to explain to others why it is worthwhile investing in the functions you carry out: you will need a special 'bag of tricks' at work.

In Chapter 3, we point to some key insights you need about your own 'work personality', how you might go about getting such insights, and how they could be crucial in helping you deal with the inevitable challenges in the workplace.

Chapter 4 addresses head-on the need to develop a professional brand and to market yourself the way any product or service is. We focus in particular on the power of professional associations as career builders.

Chapter 5 gets practical with a look at job hunting, the tools of applying for a job, interviewing, and getting safely through the critical first few weeks on a new job.

Chapter 6 outlines the building blocks of a resume and comments on the conflicting advice you may receive.

In Chapter 7, we comment on the notion that 'career planning' may be a contradiction in terms. Of course planning and skill building are essential – but there is no accounting for chance, and it is important to be ready for it.

Chapter 8 takes a look at the reality of organizational life: success is not guaranteed to the technically proficient. Political savvy is paramount! That said, simple guidelines go a long way toward reducing stress and maximizing effectiveness within an organizational culture.

In Chapter 9, we cover the essential skill of constructing compelling proposals and business cases. Regardless of the nature of the workplace (private or public sector, large or small), advocacy and getting support for change and investment requires compelling arguments.

By Chapter 10, we want to help you as you transition to a first managerial position. You do not have to make the mistakes we did!

Chapter 11 stresses the importance of the attitude we bring to our work, and we touch on the need to be honest about when it may be appropriate to leave a work situation.

Chapter 12 takes a look at salary and other aspects of compensation and suggests resources for ensuring you are armed with the relevant information at times of negotiation.

In Chapter 13, we advocate for a lifelong mentoring orientation. Take advantage of the wisdom of those older and more experienced when you are young... and pay it back, either as a young 'techie' supporting senior colleagues or as a more experienced professional guiding those looking for support.

In Chapter 14, you get a chance to hear the career stories of colleagues of ours.

In Chapter 15, we introduce ourselves and comment on the lessons we have learned through varied and rewarding careers.

We hope that by the time you have sampled our book or gone through it systematically, you will feel energized and confident about the work life still ahead of you.

2

An opaque profession: special challenges

Unlike some professionals holding well-understood occupations – think teachers, dentists, sports coaches – practitioners in information-related fields deal with a unique challenge throughout their careers: their employers and potential beneficiaries may not appreciate why it is worthwhile paying for their services:

> Had I only known how much work I'd need to do to justify my job, my department, my staff, and my budget... perhaps I would have chosen a profession everybody understands!

> It wasn't mentioned in the graduate program that selling and advocacy is in fact the key element in the job of an information professional.

> It is quite disconcerting to have senior managers – who may have no familiarity at all with what we do – comment that we are expendable now that Google takes care of our work.

> Looking back, I would have educated myself sooner about relationship management, grassroots support, and political savvy.

We hear comments like these all the time. They illustrate in personal ways a fundamental and pervasive challenge associated with our evolving profession: *outside the community of our grateful clients, few people have a clear impression of the range, impact, and value of the work information professionals do.*

Some professions are universally understood

Practitioners in well-understood professions may feel they are underpaid and overworked, but they don't usually comment that it's a mystery to others what they contribute. There may be concerns about the cost of the skilled experts who operate an MRI machine and interpret the resulting images, but no one questions the diagnostic value of their work. There may be concerns about the cost of the public school system, but no one questions the need for the teachers.

Information professionals do not generally enjoy such universal acceptance of their value and function. Similarly, they are not among the professionals called on as a matter of course when there is a problem to be dealt with. No one has any doubt the veterinarian must be seen if a pet is ill; we would all look for a roofer if rain leaks into the house; everyone knows to call the police if a crime is witnessed. We bet few have ever heard the cry 'call an information professional, pronto!'

Going a bit deeper, we could say that no one questions the *enabling* functions carried out by veterinarians, roofers, and law enforcement personnel. Of course they need to procure materials, pay for various personnel, fund computing infrastructure, and so on. Our enabling functions – procurement, cataloguing, taxonomy construction, website maintenance, and so on – may not be understood, and we may need to explain them many times (without using jargon, of course).

What do people know about what we do?

The views commonly expressed about our profession – for example, when we seek input for strategic planning – focus on a subset of activities associated with what is visible and tangible: we are known to manage a physical collection of paper records, print materials, and other items (in the case of public libraries, of videos, music, games, and art). By those who have given us 'impossible' questions, we are known as magicians who are able to dig up the most obscure information, and by those who may request more casual assistance from time to time, we are described as unfailingly courteous and responsive.

All the efforts and skills going into resource discovery and assessment, license negotiations with vendors, content management for the intranet, current awareness alerting – just to mention a few of the behind-the-scenes functions we undertake – tend to fly under the radar. As an example, the work associated with specialized taxonomies to manage corporate repositories is so remote from the awareness of most that we often find ourselves needing to describe it in lay terms when explaining the resources required to operate information functions.

But let that be OK. Let's agree that we aren't about to conduct seminars for the general public about the enabling work tasks we undertake. Those tasks are our business – and in fact we would argue that we should focus not on what we do and how we do it but on developing and presenting our value proposition: *what is the impact and value we deliver to the communities and organizations we serve?*

Fashioning the value message

Given that our value message is not universally appreciated the way other professionals' value is, we must step up and craft the message ourselves, in ways our stakeholders find meaningful. Here are some considerations:

- We have traditionally been preoccupied delivering value as opposed to collecting *evidence* of that value. We must turn our attention to such evidence collection, which is not the same thing as activity statistics!

- It is impossible to attach a financial value calculation to information services: what is the monetary value of the fact that an item in a library, archives, or museum collection turned out to be invaluable for a policy analyst, city planner, or engineer? What if it made the difference between one decision and another?

- It is equally difficult to attach a risk financial value: what is the cost when information is lacking? In some cases, we may be able to project a financial consequence of lacking or inaccurate information; for example, we can calculate the costs of extra treatment for a patient who accidentally received the wrong drug or dosage. Most of the time, we cannot assign a monetary value. For example, we can only describe in qualitative ways the impact of an analyst starting a project from scratch, unaware of the relevant information available in the library or corporate repository.

- Our value plays out over a very long time horizon. Cataloguing and protecting a report (especially a grey literature item) decades ago may turn out to be incredibly valuable today… accordingly, we need to justify investment today for future value. Mechanisms for harvesting information and the content we collect in our repositories now may pay off in unforeseen ways years down the road for people arriving in the organization long after we left.

In older times, the profession of librarianship enjoyed a more secure esteem in the views of academics, scholars, researchers, and public library users because it was clear that librarians held the keys to stored knowledge. Now, we need advocacy and salesmanship because the emergence of information saturation, search engines, and social media has driven a perception that 'everyone with access to the internet is now a researcher' and 'everything anyone wants to know is available on the internet'. Our challenge now and in the future is not to refute such perceptions as much as it is to create the experience on the part of our stakeholders how much *more* value we can deliver than the open web tools themselves are capable of delivering.

In Chapters 4 and 9, we discuss promotion – of ourselves and our projects – in more detail. But we wanted to set the stage by being honest about a key characteristic of information-related professions: not only should you expect to explain yourself if at a social gathering you are asked what you do, you should hone your skills in explaining to stakeholders and funders *throughout your career* how the information professions' practitioners deliver value worth paying for.

The corporate repository manager

A subcategory of information professionals work in roles associated with managing an organization's records – evidence of business transactions conducted, of discussions held to arrive at decisions, and the myriad other information objects arising out of conducting the affairs of the organization. The old fashioned records manager role has a long tradition, and many are the anecdotes about 'central files' being a black hole from which information could be extracted only by the one person who had operated the filing room for decades. Contemporary roles are becoming better known along with document management systems and systems to archive and search the massive volumes of email arising from day to day operations.

In regulated industries, record keeping is highly developed and those who operate the systems to manage the physical and electronic records are regarded as indispensable because the law mandates the function. Elsewhere, the need for discipline in record keeping and document and email management may be fully appreciated only when litigation hits or whistleblowers attract media attention ('what did they know and when did they know it?'). In many organizations, employees complain about the amount of time they waste trying to find documents ('does anyone know where the latest version of the Mansfield contract is?') or trace decision trails ('why did that policy get adopted two years ago?'), but the complaints about inconvenience or frustration don't add up to a six-figure investment in content management or enterprise search systems. The position of 'corporate memory keeper' simply doesn't exist, and the highly qualified information professional who could fill it loses out on a job.

The information specialist

A subcategory of information professionals – among themselves called *special librarians* for want of a more evocative common denominator – work in dedicated organizational libraries or information centers, for example in pharmaceutical companies, hospitals, government agencies, and so on. They report dealing with a particular challenge when executives decide 'we no longer need a library, we just need to keep the electronic journals'. The executives making such decisions are typically focusing on the budget cost of the library, having no direct experience with the services offered by it (they may well receive information from their staff who in turn may have obtained it from the library). Indeed, it's difficult to blame anyone for making a cost cutting decision of this nature if he or she must reduce operating and staff budgets dramatically; usually, the expectation is that no particular effect will be felt by the organization's employees because 'everyone seems to be using Google all day long' and 'everything is electronic these days'.

At the point when an executive decision has been made to close or downsize a corporate library, it may be too late for the special librarian(s) in it to convince management it is an untoward strategy. Certainly, petitions may be signed by analysts, scientists, economists, and similar knowledge workers to maintain the library, but that may not be sufficient. Management's response may be that the library has become unaffordable, period.

For these librarians, the time to rally support is every day on the job. Every interaction with knowledge workers, every reference question answered, every document procured is a must-use opportunity to explore what the impact was. The goal is to build a bridge from the often close and cordial relationships with library users to the usually weaker relationships with executives – and to 'tell the value story' in such a way as to create and sustain opinion *among managers and strategic influencers* that the library is a non-negotiable, essential corporate service.

Implications: getting used to promotional activities

Based on our experience, information professionals' careers more than likely will contain an ongoing theme of 'making the case'. In other words, they will need to pay attention to shaping a perception on the part of clients and funders that appropriate information, knowledge, and communication strategies deliver value for the investment. As examples:

- Keeping the legacy of society's history, art, architecture, and literature is a noble undertaking few would argue against. Yet when it comes to funding such work, the competition with what is seen as more immediately pressing emergencies (health care, for example) may be intense. Information professionals must publicize and demonstrate the value of their curatorial and research work in order to protect their budgets, or they may need to get involved in fund raising.

- In academic settings, the value of research and information is well understood, but budgetary pressures may squeeze the departments engaged in supplying information and tools to faculty and students. Information professionals may need to work creatively with other players in the information sphere to demonstrate the advisability of maintaining robust support.

- Now that the perception is afoot that 'the internet makes everyone a researcher', *qualified* researchers need to differentiate the value of what they find from what 'anyone' can find.

- Corporate policies and strategies for institutional memory may focus on technology solutions and overlook the need for professionals with information credentials as opposed to technology credentials. For some time, technology based approaches enjoyed a reputation as silver-bullet solutions; that is no longer the case, but information professionals need to sell themselves as possessing the best skills for addressing organizational knowledge management.

- As market conditions sharpen competition and as traditional scholarly publishing patterns change, it may be tempting for information industry players to rely on less expensive generalists. Information professionals need to show in no uncertain terms how their unique skills add value.

Show us the money: what money?

It is rare that a tangible monetary gain or savings can be attached to information and knowledge-related activities. We could ask: what is the financial value of good information, provided when it is needed, in a convenient manner, to scientists working on developing a robotics device for those with limited mobility? What is the financial value of good information practices to a police department or a city or country? But we would come up short.

Answers could range from zero to priceless, depending on a host of factors – and hindsight. But we rarely have hindsight when we need to justify investment for the future. Sure, there are standout stories of the tragic consequences of lacking information, just as there are hypothetical means of illustrating the value of knowledge ('how much would you pay to learn what is the life-saving antidote to the toxin in the berries your child just ate?').

Most information professionals are not involved in life-or-death scenarios in which no questions are asked about 'the money'. But they *are* called on to demonstrate their return on investment (not achieved by collecting activity statistics – more in Chapter 9). So they must devise ways to indicate impact: productivity gains, risk minimization, operational costs savings, protection against litigation, sharpened competitive edge, strategic market or political wins, protection of heritage, access to research results, and so on. They must produce evidence to show that something desirable and worth funding results from their work.

Information professionals will always need to do two things:

- substantiate in advance why their cost and the cost of their tools will deliver return on investment (ROI)
- show in retrospect that the ROI occurred.

That is why an important component of information professionals' work is 'outcome research': finding out and documenting what was the impact of their activities and deliverables. Such finding out involves formal audits and informal conversations ('can you tell me what difference it made that your team had the information we provided?').

News media do not question paying for information via their journalists – we see that phenomenon most clearly during elections or emergencies. Most information professionals are not routinely seen in that same light. And herein lies the special challenge.

You mean... I have to sell myself constantly?

Yes, that is what we mean. Information professionals typically need to pay constant attention to understanding the perception clients and stakeholders have of their services, and to prepare and communicate an ongoing message about the value of those services to management teams, which seem to turn over ever faster.

Some may shrink at the prospect of having to promote their services. We say, don't be modest: *information professionals' services are essential to the proper functioning of society and its organizations: if we did not exist, they'd have to invent us.*

Learning how to promote and substantiate value is the future foundation for our profession. We need to continue to work together to assist each other in that learning.

The good news: selling value by giving value

Jill and Ulla advocate this view: no one can sell anyone else on an idea or a purchase. Instead, we all can create for others an experience making them feel inclined to invest – their time or their money, or both, as the case may be. Therefore, we advocate branding that goes beyond slogans: we believe the most powerful way to demonstrate value is to create it.

Our profession may never lose its opacity – and it's immaterial whether our beneficiaries understand exactly what we do. What is essential is that they understand *the value we add to what they do.*

3

Knowing who you are: your 'work personality' and your 'best fit'

It is not a given, but most people likely will agree that career satisfaction has a lot to do with the degree to which innate characteristics and strengths match the work we do. Therefore, we invite you now – regardless whether you are still in school or have years of work behind you – to consider those innate characteristics through questions like these:

- Are you drawn to the atmosphere of a serene, luxuriously appointed law or accounting firm or to a beehive-busy college information commons?
- Does the public service or a technology startup appeal to you?
- Is working with people on top of your list, or are you happier in front of a screen by yourself?
- Would working in a unionized environment turn you off?
- Do you thrive on working fast or prefer having time to focus?
- Do you have a fondness for 'hallowed halls of history', or do you find testing the latest software tools exciting?
- Do you crave structure or freedom?

- Are you happier tearing through many specific, measurable tasks or working on somewhat loosely defined projects where your individual attainment is less discernible?

As a student or new professional, you may not know the answers, and no one expects you to! Nevertheless, we suggest that taking stock of your innate characteristics may help you target job searches and articulate your strengths in resumes and interviews. Knowing what makes you comfortable and what makes you uneasy (at least at first) will equip you to deal with many an unforeseen situation at work by enabling you to work proactively on skills you are less certain you have.

In practice, many information professionals comment how they developed a sense of their preferences only after the first or second job – in fact some say they fell into a job they knew little or nothing about yet discovered they were superbly suited for and very happy in it. Our experience echoes that observation, and we stress that taking an opportunity you may feel is unfamiliar or beyond your comfort zone could lead to new discoveries about talents you possess.

In this chapter, we explore personal work styles and preferences quite apart from professional competencies. Regardless whether you work in a technical capacity, in a client support or outreach role, or as a manager, certain personality-related preferences will influence your level of satisfaction and pride at work.

Graduate school may not provide opportunities for career soul searching, but we strongly recommend getting very clear about work personality – even though we know your top priority out of school may simply be to obtain a job that pays a living wage! Whether you are pondering the next career step or assessing longer-term directions (say, academic versus private sector versus government), consider the potential match between your preferences and interests on the one hand and typical work environments on the other.

Once past the first job, don't count on happenstance although it may be a powerful factor – instead be deliberate about aiming for types of organization and types of role most likely to match your personal work style preferences.

Examples of work personalities

One friend's work personality
Systematic and methodical. Dislikes interruptions and sudden changes. Similarly dislikes noisy, disordered environments. Likes to have ample time to complete work and prefers sequential rather than simultaneous tasks. Appreciates long range schedules. Uncomfortable with ambiguity. Spends extra time making sure every detail is correct. Takes pride in perfection and completeness and easily gets flustered if questioned. Happier working alone than in a team. Finds it stressful when needing to coordinate activities with multiple people. Easily adapts to direction and formal procedures. Plans well and meets deadlines. Desk and cubicle extremely tidy and impersonal.

Even with this abbreviated description, it is relatively easy to conjure up functions and environments that would suit our friend perfectly – and ones that would not!

Another friend's work personality
Thrives on starting new projects and learning new things. Goes with the flow and copes well with change and surprises. Easily bored with routine. Happiest working with a group of creative people. Enjoys interaction and welcomes impromptu meetings. Finds it a chore to tie up loose ends and complete documentation. Not worried about typos. Typically has a number of projects on the go at any one time. Finds it annoying when rules or structure inhibit latitude. Big picture approach with high tolerance for ambiguity and approximation. Creative and curious, often expressing frustration at official regulations. Is challenged to meet deadlines. Desk and cubicle 'artistically enhanced'.

You guessed it: our second friend would love the types of roles and places our first friend would detest!

On the surface, it could appear that the functions in the information professions – research, content management, cataloguing and indexing, documentation and database management, web and intranet-related work, curating and archiving, and publishing – are sufficiently similar to point to a fairly narrow range of personality types. The reality is more complex, especially as technology and society evolves to create new job functions. A more nuanced assessment of work preferences is called for.

Work preferences are personal

Our individual personalities influence how we react to surroundings, how much stress or contentment we experience in response to events or circumstances, and what types of activities are attractive to us. Below, we discuss several aspects of what constitutes a good workplace fit. Knowing what makes you anxious, content, stressed, proud, and so on is a helpful pointer when you are assessing options for your future.

Consider how comfortable you believe you would feel performing the following tasks typical for information professionals:

- responding to a request for background information for a meeting starting in 30 minutes – a meeting that will make or break a six or seven figure deal
- preparing a briefing report summarizing the current scientific thinking in a controversial matter for the purposes of a meeting three months from now
- managing a short-staffed intranet team whose members' patience is wearing thin

- preparing the public library's budget and work plan and defending it in front of a city council eager to slash costs
- setting up and conducting sales meetings with long standing customers of software or content who are indicating budgets are being reduced
- convincing potential customers of a brand new product or service that they would benefit from attending a product demonstration
- leading a team investigating options for an enterprise search solution
- cataloguing and indexing a historical collection of rare and precious materials
- organizing the move to new storage facilities for extremely fragile and irreplaceable items requiring, for example, low light and temperature control
- developing a mobile delivery and support project for an academic institution moving into distance education in a big way
- pioneering the use of social networking tools among teams of knowledge workers
- creating a taxonomy of the 'correct way to name things and topics' for an enterprise content management and search initiative
- conducting training sessions for college students to orient them about the offerings of the academic library
- conducting training sessions for policy analysts, accountants, lawyers, engineers, scientists, and other knowledge workers to orient them about the offerings of the corporate information center
- managing the records department in a public entity subject to freedom-of-information requests

- spearheading the implementation of a new document or content management system unwelcome among employees who are not aware of its benefits

- staffing a trade show booth in a marketing and sales role

- making substantive public presentations at conferences in an advocacy role.

Our fundamental approach to work vs. personal life

Just as we all have a unique personality, we all have a unique approach to work. Consider the following example statements as a way of jogging your ideas about your approach to work and career:

> I work in a respectable occupation and although I don't find it exciting, I provide for my family.

> I am deeply invested in what I'm doing at work and worry about it all the time.

> On weekends, I find myself longing to get back to work on Monday because my project is so interesting and exciting.

> Some mornings, I don't know how I'm going to make it through the day because of the boredom/stress/uncertainty/workload/politics, and I'm looking high and low for any way to get out of here.

> My eye is on my next job, even if I am happy in my current one. I want to advance as high as I can in my career.

Rank and title is less of a concern for me – I want to move things along and make a difference.

I take pride in always meeting my deadlines and performing my work with zero mistakes.

I will go into the office on weekends and pull all-nighters if necessary – and I have. I can be reached at any time by my colleagues if they need help, and I check email in the evening and on weekends just in case something needs attention.

My work does not require my attention in overtime or during my holidays; I am entitled to be, and appreciate being, out of reach during non-office hours.

I love being where the action is.

I appreciate the fact that nothing can happen to my materials or alter the state of my projects while I am away from work.

My colleagues are a significant element in my social environment. We take an interest in each other.

Financial security is more important to me than how interesting the job is or what my title is.

I like the idea that I can stay in a job for a long time without having to take courses or learn new things.

I am active in my professional association even though my employer does not support it – so I participate in my own time and pay my own way to conferences.

I want to go back to school to make a radical change in my career.

Questions to ponder

The above example statements illustrate a range of attitudes to how we earn a living. As you no doubt detected, they reflect varying degrees of engagement and ambition – approaches range from 'I go to work to pay for the non-work aspects of my life – now and in retirement' to 'my work *is* my life'. Stressing that no value judgments are implied, and that our attitudes to work evolve over time, we invite you to consider now the following questions – your answers will offer clues to types of work you may find appealing or unattractive and thus to directions you may choose in graduate studies or continuing education:

- Do you look at work as a means to finance everything else you do?

- Do you define yourself by who you are in private life – in your non-work hours – or by what you do? (If you are not sure, visualize having no job or professional role at all.)

- When someone asks you what you do, are you proud and eager or hesitant and apologetic when you answer?

- Do you value – or believe you would value in the future – the kind of job you can 'leave behind' when the work day is over so you don't take work or stress home?

- Are you engaged in your profession outside work, for example by belonging to and being active in volunteer groups or associations, writing articles, or the like?

- Are you striving to find your special niche where your innate and learned skills will generate significant value for others?

- Are you unsure what your greatest talent is… and therefore unsure which vocational direction to take?

- Do you have ambitions about being well known among your peers?

- How much tolerance do you have for work-related events causing changes of plans or timing in your private life?

- Looking back now to when you graduated, would you do something different when you were applying for jobs?

- Looking back now over the jobs you have had, would you change anything about your approach to work or about how you prioritized work versus your private life – and if so, what would the change be?

Implications for types of environments

Information professionals generally work in an environment we would characterize as 'office', 'professional' or 'academic'. Still, our work environments differ, and according to the above points we may have narrower or broader tolerances when it comes to the types of environments in which we feel at ease. Any setting – public, private, non-profit – may involve a mix of features such as calm and rush... but it's worth considering which ones may be desirable or challenging if there is a preference.

For example, an immigrant settlement organization and an engineering firm would likely present very different work environments, just as a college resource center and a city archives would appeal to some and not to others. You may have a desire to work in a 'plush' environment, or you may care little about your physical space. It's a personal preference and priority, but we mention it here because it has an influence on work satisfaction.

The source of professional satisfaction: what makes you happy?

We recognize that through university you may not have a clear picture of the type of accomplishment that would give you a kick. After all, university work differs significantly from professional work. Still, we believe there are hints throughout our formative years as to what will make us happy and what will turn us off. We illustrate some types of situations professionals say give them satisfaction. Yes, of course, it is satisfying to earn a good salary and to advance through the ranks... but here we are looking at the types of situations that make you *delighted and proud*.

Which of the comments below resonate as something you would like to say in a future work role?

- 'It delights me when the students come around to give me the thumbs up that my guidance helped them nail their assignments.'

- 'It is hugely satisfying when the analysts tell management how they could not have tackled the project without my team in the information center.'

- 'Getting all those maps indexed into the system so fast was our contribution, and it saved the day so the launch date was met!'

- 'My team ensured the high-profile project's managers had all they needed to consider the options and it was gratifying to hear them mention it publicly.'

- 'Project managing the move of the archives to the new facility was a daunting challenge – but I'm thrilled to say I delivered!'

- 'Through sheer determination and increasing competence as I went along, I have been able to get through a huge backlog of documents needing processing.'

- 'As a sales and customer service representative, I take pride in the fact that my clients trust me to give them the best advice.'

- 'Getting the budget increase approved was an incredible achievement!'

- 'It was exhilarating to give that presentation to so many people!'

- 'Through my team's efforts, the best enterprise search solution was identified and selected, and the users are very pleased.'

- 'The website overhaul was much more labor intensive than I thought, but I persisted and I'm proud to say the end result is getting great feedback.'

- 'I knew when to seek outside help – fortunately – so in the end I delivered the best result for the organization.'

- 'The new software product is getting rave reviews, and I had something to do with it through my work on the interface.'

- 'It's a terrific feeling to know I helped the customer select the best option from among the possible choices – I know I earned a lot of trust by not just pushing the most expensive one.'

Your red flags: what would frustrate you?

In a similar way, we are honest about the fact that some aspects of working life and day to day situations may bother us. No job is perfectly attuned to any one person's preferences, but it would be untoward to take a position whose nature could offer more triggers for stress than another would. Hence we turn your attention now to some questions aimed at *situations and circumstances* that may feel unpleasant for you, depending on your personal inclination:

- Do you experience stress when things don't move as fast as you would like them to?

- Would you find it stressful to work on committees because of their tendency to bog down?

- Would you be uncomfortable in a highly regulated environment where deviation and creativity is not feasible?

- Does an extremely busy and volatile environment make you anxious?

- Are you likely to feel bored in a job with lots of routine?

- Would you burn out in a position where lack of resources made it necessary for you to turn down requests from clients?

- Would you dread a workday filled with clients requesting assistance from you 'yesterday if not sooner'?

- Does the idea of providing opinion and advice make you cringe because you fear you could be wrong?

- Do you fear having to reveal lack of knowledge, as in asking a client 'what does that acronym mean'?

- Is it daunting to prepare budget request justifications and business cases – never mind presenting to a management team in person?

- Would it cause you stress to straddle between client expectations and reality, having to say, in essence, 'no' or 'not until May'?

- Is dealing with administrivia something you instinctively find unappealing?

- Are you worried about making mistakes as the manager of a team because the role requires a great deal of interpersonal finesse you aren't sure you have?

Your natural role

According to our personalities and to the sources of our professional satisfaction or stressors, we tend to take on and be comfortable in certain roles in the work environment. Knowing what roles suit us may offer some helpful clues when it comes to making career choices. You may recognize yourself or your colleagues in these descriptions of common workplace roles.

Over our careers, we may move from one to another role and back again, just as we may exhibit characteristics of several roles depending on the team or project we are working on.

Leaders or instigators

Regardless whether they have a management position, leaders or instigators seem incapable of keeping a low profile, always stepping up to take on a new project, organizing special events such as an 'information fair' for employees, or running a charity drive at work. They are 'idea people', frequently making suggestions for improvements, new services or products, or new ways to accomplish tasks. On their own initiative, they may investigate new tools and introduce them to colleagues. They are usually energetic people who are always prepared to go the extra mile. Outside work, they join associations and groups and quickly end up in leadership roles. Often gregarious, they tend to have large social networks and are known to come through when someone asks 'do you know anyone who...'. Many leaders contribute to their profession by writing, teaching, and speaking at conferences.

Go-to persons or fixers

These are the 'local heroes' who support their team mates through their willingness to assist when difficulties arise. Often experts at a particular system or tool, they help colleagues who are new in the area, and it's typical for them to end up with the most difficult cases to work on or the truly complex glitches to fix. The role may imply some career risk in that fixers can spend so much time helping others informally that they fall behind in their own tasks – and managers may not be aware of the compensating activity so performance evaluations suffer. Fixers may be content in their role staffing an informal help desk and may prefer technical or scientific work to managerial work – they are the 'senior scientists' who are just as happy not to need to deal with personnel issues. Some fixers are also leaders.

Troops

Troops are the employees all managers dream of having. Steady as they go, they just keep performing reliably and consistently and can always be counted on to perform no matter what. Nothing fazes them, and like the fixers they aren't afraid to do some overtime or weekend work to meet a deadline. They focus on the job and don't let distractions interfere. Appreciating the stability of a secure job, they are comfortable with routine and aren't particularly competitive or concerned about status or title.

Mentors

Wise advisors or mentors may have any of the above roles and in addition perform a counseling and guidance function.

Typically midway or senior in their careers, or retired, they draw on many years of professional experience to respond to requests for their opinions in a variety of career-related situations. They may be well-known individuals with high professional profiles so it's easy to conclude they may be worth seeking out; or they may be talked up within an organization by those who have benefited from their advice – 'oh, you should speak to Anne about that'.

Developing your personal skills: a growth plan

Most professionals experience comfort in some aspects of a work situation, and the opposite in others. What is a piece of cake for one person may be a stressor for another. No value judgments can be attached to person A's ease in working with new software or person B's unease at seeing a long queue of requests for assistance. However, we are all in a position to devote effort toward building skills. That said, we are aware of opinions that professionals ought not to obsess about weaknesses to the detriment of strengths. We agree that there is no point in trying to remake ourselves and ignore the innate talents we do have. Let's leverage to the utmost our top strengths and be aware of areas where seeking advice or assistance might be advisable.

If you discover skill areas that need to be refined or enhanced, or situations you need to master, don't consider it a negative but rather a welcome challenge that will help you grow professionally. Examples of situations potentially inducing uncertainty include:

- handling day to day surprises or sudden changes of organizational direction
- staying calm in the face of high-volume and constant demand for your attention
- prioritizing tasks for a limited time frame and tolerating a backlog of unfinished tasks
- being patient with organizational process or committee work
- understanding the nature of interpersonal dynamics and departmental politics
- constantly having to learn new technologies and tools
- dealing with needy, demanding, or otherwise 'difficult' people
- feeling insecure in a managerial role
- speaking formally to groups and larger audiences
- writing reports for wider distribution
- preparing formal proposals
- 'asking for the sale' or pitching a new product in a vendor role
- ... and many more.

Should you experience a vague sense of discomfort or anxiety associated with such situations or with other aspects in your studies or work, without being able to put your finger on its source, we recommend a brief foray into the realm of personality analysis. The internet offers many free personality tests from which you may draw conclusions about situations that may put you on edge; those tests are a good start for your skills development plan.

What can you do? Plenty!

We are blessed to live and work in societies offering a plethora of educational opportunities for personal development, and many are the books and seminars available to everyone. Any visit to a bookseller will reveal the richness of materials to guide us in the world of work and life balance, people skills, time management, and so on. From the pragmatic to the more esoteric, the range of items from which to choose is your opportunity to find something that resonates with you. As for seminars, workshops, and motivational speech events, there is a similar abundance – in part because the field of life coaching is growing fast. A tried and true example is Toastmasters; colleagues have told us they gained precious confidence by taking the program. We believe every information professional will be drawn naturally to exploring the resources... after all, that's our specialty!

Beyond taking in the lessons in books and seminars privately, there are opportunities to seek input and guidance from interaction with others (we cover some aspects when we discuss mentoring later on in Chapter 13). It is understandable that you may not wish to reveal a sense of weakness by, say, going to human resources. Seeking out colleagues in other organizations who may have insights to share (this is where belonging to associations comes in) is a rich avenue for safe inquiry.

The key is for all information professionals to be aware of 'comfort areas' and leverage strengths while being alert to opportunities for growth.

Finding the perfect work: Ulla

My first two casual high school jobs were cleaning in a bakery and tutoring French verb conjugations. Each provided its own job satisfaction: in the former, I enjoyed the sight of the clean and orderly counters, racks, and baking sheets, and imagined the bakers doing the same; in the latter, I took pride when my 'tutee' mastered the irregulars. Only recently did it occur to me that they are perfect illustrations of key elements in what makes me happy.

I have always been a neat freak and perfectionist when it comes to cleanliness – and I'm painfully uncomfortable in noisy, crowded, and 'rough' places. Hence the appeal of library school – my time at the university library certainly had been peaceful. My role as teacher had been established in third grade when I helped my best friend who struggled with reading, so guidance to others would be natural.

A summer job during university illustrated other personal traits: I can't stand anything sloppy or incorrect, and I crave the freedom to do something about it. My job was to prepare one of the day's meals for patients in a long-term care facility, arraying customized sandwiches on trays according to individual directions (no salt, no crust, white bread only, and so on). My guide was a hand written, much overscrawled list with all the appearance of having been around a while. I found it extremely challenging to 'translate' from the messy list to the physical reality of bread, butter, and slices of ham. Forthwith, I prepared color-coded visual 'tray maps', slipped them into plastic sleeves, and affixed them on the wall above my work area – much to the kitchen manager's astonishment and admiration!

In library school, then, what did I know about my preferences for a job after graduation? I knew I was looking for an orderly, organized, manageable environment in which I had some control and could shape documentation and other work instruments to my liking. Lucky for me, the office in which I served as assistant to the director of the library school fit that bill. Though less orderly and subject to significant workload variations, my next work environment still allowed me huge scope for taking charge of customer service, customer seminar planning, etc. 'my way'. No one interfered in the way I kept the schedules on the wall or how I stacked in-trays 12 high to keep papers in order. And no one interfered when I worked hundreds of hours of overtime, either!

The latitude to decide how to carry out the responsibilities associated with satisfying the customers was a godsend. It was fun to investigate system or billing glitches and get to the bottom of why and how something happened – so it could be rectified for the future. It was wonderful to craft a new seminar, deliver it, and get superb feedback. Most of all, it was delightful to know I was trusted to do the right thing. Add to all this the fact that I got to teach much of the time – formally in seminars delivered to customers and informally to colleagues. I could not have conjured up in my imagination a more perfect work situation, and the experience is what enables me to discuss career choices with others.

Working with the company's customers, and since 1992 with my own clients, I have encountered workplaces exhibiting constraints I would have difficulty feeling good about. I would likely find it frustrating to deal with the many rules and regulations characteristic of workplaces under public scrutiny, and I'm certain it would be a source of stress for me to be forced to stint on service as a result of staff and budget limitations typical in many settings. So it's a happy outcome for me that I could set up my own practice: I am the most demanding boss I ever had – but I'm secure in the knowledge that what I do for my clients is appreciated. (As for the noise thing: believe me, it's extremely quiet in my home office, and *I'm* in charge of the cleaning and tidying!)

Discovering the real me: Jill

The 'me' who went to work when I was in my 20s was a woman who liked challenges and new opportunities as well as being part of the 'troops'. I enjoyed small, limited leadership roles but didn't see myself as a l-e-a-d-e-r. Thankfully, the limited leadership roles did teach me that I could be a leader if necessary, even if it wasn't what I wanted. When I was given the opportunity to take training to be a supervisor, I grabbed it. At least then I knew better what to do if the opportunity arose... and it did!

In my 20s and early 30s, I was willing to put in extra hours, but also enjoyed my non-work hours. For example, work allowed me to pay for interesting trips and opportunities to expand my horizons. Life was good and it was well rounded.

In my early 30s, I went from being an important member of the troops to being a supervisor and manager. I was in charge of services, people, budgets, and more. While I had worked on stressful projects, the new role provided a different level of stress. I was ultimately responsible for things that sometimes seemed out of my control. I had to learn how to delegate and communicate better. I had to pay attention to more details. And sometimes I had to put work first – before fun.

Zoom ahead to my early 40s. I still liked challenges and new opportunities. I had been a successful leader, but also had functioned as part of the team when workloads demanded it. I had been in very stressful work situations and finally realized that I needed to be more in control of my own destiny. After nearly a year of soul searching, learning, obtaining advice, and gathering resources, I quit working for someone else and started a consulting practice.

All of my work life, even going back to when I was a teenager, I would get up early and likely be one of the first people to the office. I defined myself as a morning person although I wouldn't necessarily engage in deep conversation before 8 a.m. After I had been working for myself for a while, I discovered the real me is really a night person. I often do my best work in the evenings. I've grown more fully into being a leader, but recognize that I can help others learn how to lead by stepping aside to let them step up and by supporting them in their efforts. And I've continued to recognize and foster the part of me that likes challenges and new opportunities. That part keeps me jazzed, excited, and interested in what I do.

Along the way, I have read, taken classes, sought the advice of others, and been willing to walk out on more thin ice than you can imagine. All of it has helped me learn who I am. I know I get my energy from being by myself. I can be extroverted when the situation calls for it but really value 'alone time'. I like to have information to use when making decisions, but often go with gut and intuition. I can be very decisive. I learn by doing and by 'getting my hands dirty'. I can absorb a tremendous amount of information in a wide variety of ways. I like technology and can learn it quickly. With it, I live on the leading but not on the 'bleeding' edge. Finally, I am a person who is comfortable taking small and big risks.

Developing your brand: the professional image

We hear you thinking, 'what, I have a brand?', and we answer, 'everyone does!' Of course we don't mean to imply an information professional's brand is the equivalent of brands associated with global consumer products. We are persons and not watches or vehicles, so our brands do not carry associations of, say, status or wealth the way a Rolex or a Rolls-Royce would; instead our brands are entirely tied to our *value at work*. We all possess a collection of qualities making us uniquely recognizable, employable, and valuable. *The critical mass of knowledge or perceptions others have about what we do and how well we do it adds up to a brand.*

In developing our brands and selling ourselves to employers or clients, the focus is on questions such as: What do we bring to the table that is uniquely desirable in the work place or project? What influence has our work had on the group of stakeholders we serve – or on a wider community such as a professional association?

What would be the earmarks of a strong professional brand? Let's say it exists when:

- an employer starting to review a resume exclaims, 'Oh, I've heard of her!'

- colleagues in the workplace seek his input regardless of whether he's involved in the project

- colleagues in other organizations refer to her by first name as a subject authority
- conference attendees flock to hear him speak because of what they have heard about his presentations
- she's approached regularly to nominate candidates for elected office in an association.

In other words, there is *awareness* about the person's abilities, competence, contributions to the profession, and so on. In the discipline of marketing, the extensive and fascinating body of literature about brands can be highly recommended as a source of inspiration for the development of the professional brands attached to our names.

Our brands are closely associated with the images people form in their minds when they think of us. Naturally, each of our audiences have unique views of our activities – the students with whom we share our experience see us from a different angle than our employers and clients do – so it would be fair to say we all have multiple brands or variations of an overall brand.

Similarly, our brands change as we gain experience. The recent graduate's brand of 'energetic new professional up on the latest web tools' could morph over the years into 'highly respected expert in federated search' and then into 'strong manager running a large IT department'.

Do you know how others see you?

If you are unsure what impression your co-workers, manager, and professional peers have of you, you may need to take a deep breath and ask! You could be pleasantly surprised to find others perceive you as you would like to be perceived... or intrigued to find out how you are *in fact* seen!

In her talks about career matters, Ulla shares an anecdote about how she discovered by accident, early in her career, the assumptions made by a few colleagues because she 'walked fast, talked fast, and used a lot of Kleenex'. (Yes, that would describe an energetic individual with allergies, but not necessarily a drug addict!) She adds that over time she has similarly become acutely aware how a professional's focus and tenacity may be perceived by others as a pushy attitude.

During Jill's first semester teaching at Syracuse University, she discovered that other faculty in her program thought she was a technologist. In fact, one of her library science faculty colleagues started to explain library science to her! She has never found out what it is about her – dress, attitude, use of language – but Jill appears to come across first as a business person who loves technology, then as an information professional.

Since we stumbled on evidence of others' impressions, we have been conscious about the reputation we appear to have, and we attempt to help others manage their reputations. Let us illustrate, by drawing on decades of conversations with colleagues and peers, comments that often surprise the individuals they describe:

- 'It's uncanny the way she finds information no one else can find.'
- 'He's unmatched in his artistry with websites.'
- 'She has a natural knack for resolving complexity.'
- 'He deals sensitively and effectively with clients who have special needs.'
- 'No one is more generous with her time.'
- 'If it's the latest gadget, he's already the expert.'
- 'She acts as a professional match maker, always introducing colleagues in her huge network.'
- 'His vision and ability to inspire is legendary.'

The core of our brand: the value we offer, the difference we make

Quickly, what *value* do you offer an employer? You have 10 seconds!

Many of our younger colleagues are stumped – at least for some time – when we ask that question. Through conversation, they typically arrive at a formulation they feel comfortable going off to elaborate on – but it's striking how difficult many professionals find the task of articulating their value.

A slightly easier question may be: what *difference* do you make? Through it, we invite contemplation of not just 'how would the workplace fare if I weren't around?' but also and more critically 'how do my specific actions impact the workplace and the clients?' Here are some illustrative answers:

I made or make a difference because I...:

- was uniquely responsible for the most-visited exhibit in the city museum's history
- led the project to digitize the documents from the department's archive
- orchestrated the move to the new facility and built a new visitor's center
- trained the staff to perform client service at a much higher level
- devised the mechanism for converting the legacy spreadsheets into the current database
- am where the buck stops if clients have difficulties
- respond instantly when the journalists need data and fact checking within minutes

- proactively support the vice principal, who is often challenged in public
- reliably dig through mountains of documentation to identify what the auditors need
- investigate the new tools in the marketplace and recommend strategies to the IT group
- regularly develop proposals for streamlining operations to save resources
- have patiently built relationships with city administrators to the benefit of the library.

Choosing a brand: rely on natural strengths

Judging by our experience and that of our colleagues, we would say a brand develops naturally over time, on a foundation of particular strengths and talents, as opposed to being designed or conceived deliberately. Such a natural emergence of a brand does not preclude conscious attention to fostering a particular impression among those who could be our future employers or offer recommendations to them.

Just as we may come to occupy certain roles according to our personal traits, so too our brands are likely to be extensions of innate tendencies. If so, they will be easy to sustain; it would be more difficult to create and maintain a brand requiring constant striving. For example, a new professional might look around and conclude that 'the latest technology' is where it's at and desire to fashion a professional brand emphasizing technological expertise – but if such a brand is not supported by a genuine personal interest, much effort may lie ahead. Conversely, a brand resting on 'what comes naturally' will maintain itself for that very reason.

Supporting a brand: reputation and visibility in traditional and new media

Given how a brand cannot exist without the awareness of potential employers or recommenders, it is obvious that we need to work on getting noticed in positive ways. We all want to be in front of the right people, virtually or in person.

The effort starts with a basic examination: what journals, magazines, blogs, tweets, and video clips are being read and seen by the people you hope will form a positive impression of you?

Then, we advise: get out your virtual pencil and start writing. Seek out guidance from others with more experience... but make it a habit to offer insights, pointers, and (we all hope) useful commentary to the professional community – starting, if you are still a student, with the social media groups or discussion groups associated with your class or faculty. Ideally, pick a subject niche and build up a critical mass of postings to demonstrate you know what you are talking about, and – if you find it appropriate to the image you want to project – show you are a reliable source of references to new developments in the niche.

We guarantee that the newsletter editors of professional associations will be grateful for your offer to contribute. Seek out local community groups publishing newsletters – likely there's an 'information angle' relevant to the group. For example, a local school may be undertaking an innovative project using social media that would be right up your alley.

One way to get started writing pieces for publication is to prepare book reviews of non-mainstream works and local events. Publishers may be willing to supply an on-loan review copy, or you may have to wait until the local public library carries an item (but in the case of local interest material, your access would be straightforward). Museum exhibits and events of interest to the readership of a newsletter or local newspaper could be described, and the organizers may be thrilled with the publicity.

In the case of community events, you may consider a video side line. Why not offer the local art museum, a job fair organizer, or a local charity the opportunity to be featured in a clip on the internet?

Once you are comfortable having produced a body of publications, blog posts, or videos, you may feel ready and qualified for 'the live stage'. We recognize up front that not everyone is interested in nor comfortable with performing in real time, but for visibility, it's worth offering to local organizations a talk on subjects of interest. The pitfalls of social media is but one topic many local organizations might have wanted to feature for their members when Facebook first took off!

Each and every item that deals with a professional topic and has your name on it adds to your credibility and visibility.

Professional associations: key to brand building

Just as you want to be in front of the right eyeballs through your written contributions, so you want to be 'in the room' with the people who could matter in furthering your career. Again, it's a basic question: those people you want to impress... where do they congregate (in person or virtually)?

We cannot overemphasize the value of being active in the appropriate professional association. We mince no words: *it is a must* – from student days on. Please be aware that some associations offer student memberships at very affordable rates; such bargains are a wonderful means of entering into a community of professionals.

Professional associations are the perfect venue for growing professionally in a completely safe and accepting environment. Fellow members share your interest in professional growth, and any little mishaps are usually addressed by a collegial 'next time, why don't you...'. You may even experience that a fellow member takes you aside for some in-depth advice. We discuss mentoring later; our key message here is that you simply must belong to and be active in the associations regarded as relevant by your future employers. The month-in, month-out opportunity to be in the room with and conversing virtually with people who could impact your career is simply not to be passed up.

The very fact that you stick your neck out in a professional association speaks well of you to potential employers even if they do not personally attend or have friends who encountered you at the meetings.

Ah, you say: what should I offer to do? We answer: you have the opportunity to volunteer for any number of roles – including writing for an association's publications; summaries of events are popular. If you are uncertain what role you may want to offer to assume, begin with something straightforward like handling event registration and name tags. Such a seemingly simple function will allow you to shake hands and exchange a few words with everyone attending an event – getting to know them and letting them get to know you. Soon enough, you may be approaching or writing to someone saying, 'we met briefly at a meeting of the X Association, I was the one at the reception table'. Discussion list management and website maintenance are similar obvious low-fear roles to get you started.

Be sure to build on your early roles; make it a practice never to be without a function in your chosen association. You may not at the outset aspire to be president but we invite you to ponder: did not the well-known association presidents start out as students or junior members just the way you did?

Having an association role gives you a carte blanche for approaching a wide range of individuals, each time presenting yourself as a consummate professional. Here some examples of what you might say:

> I am the events coordinator for the X chapter of Y Association and would be grateful if we could discuss…
>
> As the editor of the bulletin (or blog) for X Association, I am seeking your input on…
>
> As the student liaison with the Faculty of X, I seek your support regarding…
>
> I am coordinating a student practicum volunteer program and hereby offer you…
>
> I am leading a team of student investigators and…
>
> Following on the recent X conference, the editorial team for our association newsletter would appreciate your approval of the attached summary of your speech.

As you mature, you will be expected to assume committee chair roles, interest group or section chair roles, and so on, until you are asked by a nominating committee to run for election to the board. It is a progression no different from the rise in responsibility you expect in your employment.

Everything you do in your association is a free advertisement and brand promotion. Just do it – and verify that your colleagues regard your efforts with respect. One signal of such regard is being asked to do more tasks!

What if no one has heard of me?

You may well be thinking: what if I'm applying for a position far away from my local networks and no one reading my resume is likely to have heard of me? Good question.

Our answer focuses on bringing your brand into the resume, social networking profile, or online application in several ways:

- Engaging language unique to your abilities and offerings: your written representation – and we do recognize the written word is a poor substitute for a person in the flesh – should reflect as clearly as possible the unique qualities and skills that make you the professional you are. (That's why we counsel against trite generalities like 'excellent communication skills' meaning exactly nothing because they can mean anything.)
- Story telling: your description should include a succinct 'story' about a difference or impact you have had.
- References to your professional engagement in associations and the community: showing your extracurricular professional work paints a picture of someone who contributes 'over and above'.
- Mastery of the formulation: through correct, consistent, and elegant language you have an opportunity to send a signal about your professionalism. Every word, turn of phrase, item of punctuation, header, and bullet is an opportunity to let your competence shine through (just as even one misplaced apostrophe sends an opposite message).

We discuss resumes in more detail in Chapter 6.

Professional demeanor: it's all about confidence

Information professionals are sometimes up against unfortunate old stereotypes and must counter them by acting in ways to support an image projecting 'business equal'. Many of our colleagues have shared with us how they sense they are not taken seriously by those not familiar with their roles and contributions, saying 'those receiving our direct support are delighted with what we offer, but decision makers several levels up appear to regard us as dispensable and expensive leftovers from earlier times'.

In every organizational culture, there is a 'right' set of behaviors considered to be appropriate internally and vis à vis external clients and stakeholders. Those behaviors encompass personal encounters such as meetings as well as virtual encounters occurring via social media, text messages, or email. Regardless of the means by which we are seen by others, we can't go wrong by adhering to simple guidelines.

When participating in a meeting:

- Err on the side of caution and lean to the more formal of the options available. For example, shake the hand of anyone you haven't met before and introduce yourself: 'I'm Karen Masina, in charge of the intranet. I haven't had the pleasure of meeting you until now.'

- Be punctual. It's better to wait outside someone's office or a meeting room for a minute than to rush in after the scheduled time. (We are aware that in some cultures, lateness is prevalent. Don't adopt such rude behavior.)

- Bring neatly organized materials in a suitable folder.

- Avoid excessive 'rustling' with your papers, doodling, tapping, or similar distracting tics.

- If you take notes in hand, ensure you have a tidy notebook and good pen.

- If you use a laptop or other device, ensure it's not intrusive for others.

- Come prepared, having read any agendas or background materials issued in advance. It is disrespectful to make it plain you didn't make time to prepare.

- Never engage in 'side conversations'. Raise a hand to get the meeting chair's attention if need be.

- Pay close attention to the chair and the discussion of the meeting. No matter how bored you may feel, do not engage in obviously unrelated activity (e.g. checking your messages or reading files).

- Keep the body language in check; no rolling eyes or gestures of disapproval no matter what you think of what was just said. A deadpan 'I'm sorry, I don't quite understand' is professional and yet conveys that a statement does not have your acceptance. On the other hand, a raised thumb to show support or congratulations would sometimes be just right.

When interacting virtually:

- Construct a brief virtual signature so that your function and services are always precisely identified.

- Perfect the art of 'rich subject lines' so that readers need not puzzle over what your email or blog post is about. (In fact, some messages consist of nothing but the subject line if it's clear – as in '2 p.m. meeting moved to room 334'.)

- In longer written messages, organize the material so that the *purpose and actions expected of the reader* are spelled out up front: 'This message explains the proposed course of action in the matter of X. Your answers to the questions below are requested by close of business Friday May 10.'

- Hone your writing skills to produce concise and clear text that is easy for busy readers to understand. Eradicate grammatical errors, jargon, and sloppy constructions requiring readers to work in order to follow the flow of your message. Opt for direct, simple, and active language and avoid faddish expressions without a clear and commonly accepted meaning.

■ Keep your virtual door open through offers of continued or followup service: 'I would be pleased to provide additional material if you let me know your interest.'

Economy of words

When so much of our communication is virtual, clarity and elegance of writing are paramount. The texts below illustrate how simplicity and economy of words are always preferable:

1. There are many employees that are complaining about the intranet, being confusing and difficult to use. [Here, the employees are confusing and difficult to use – and please, 'that' should not be used to refer to persons!]
2. Many employees say the intranet is confusing and difficult to use.

1. Please do not hesitate to reply to Peter or myself. This matter is very important to us and we hope that you will let him or I know about your concerns both in person and in writing.
2. Please get back to Peter and me. We are focused on the situation and hope to hear from you – come visit us or send a message.

1. Work overload is a common challenge. This leads to stress and therefore, errors get made. Customers are understandably unhappy about this. This is a concern to management, and therefore there's a project being started to address this. Those that are interested in participating are invited to a meeting about this, next Tuesday March 14.
2. Stress-inducing work overload may cause errors leading – understandably – to customer dissatisfaction. Management is starting a project to examine ways to reduce overload and hence minimize errors. Interested parties are invited to a project meeting Tuesday March 14.

Get the grammar right: a few examples to scare you

Note to readers in countries where a language other than English is used: every language is riddled with opportunities for error. Ensure your written 'trails' never contain any!

Although it is true that attitudes toward correct language usage may be fairly relaxed in some settings, you would do well to stick to 100% error free language. Readers may not form a negative impression of you over a grammatical error, but why run the risk?

Determine never to join the ranks of those who don't seem to understand the difference between...

- *their*, *there*, and *they're*
- *your* and *you're*
- *it's* and *its* [and, heaven help us, *its'*]
- *principle* and *principal*
- *faze* and *phase*

[plus hundreds of similar examples!]
.... and who don't seem to be aware of the problem in these sentences:

- As our best customer, we are offering a new premium service.
- As a celebrated artist, the audience gave him a standing ovation.
- The input you provided to Susan and I was very helpful.
- If you would like to attend, the restaurant is located at the corner of...
- My colleague Iris is more experienced than me, so I would like to refer her to you...
- We have launched a new portal which offers access to...

[plus hundreds of similar examples!]

The bottom line? We are information professionals. We look it up.

Professional polish: appearance matters

It's said that 'the care you take of your appearance signals the care you take of your work and your clients'. Amen. The same goes for the bag you carry and what's in it.

The 'dress for success' theme is well covered in a multitude of sources and the time to review the basic rules is well invested. Any visit to a local or virtual bookstore is likely to yield a book worth browsing through, and even a quick look will reassure you the rules are simple and easy to remember when shopping for or updating a work wardrobe. Below, we cover the basics of can't-fail dress code guidelines for the types of environments in which information professionals work.

The key factor in deciding on a sartorial style is whether the job function is client facing or 'back office'. Client facing roles – say, ones in sales, client training, trade show exhibits, and other front line activity – require a more formal attire than do back office ones, however there are many anecdotes from professionals who say they feel better on the job when they dress appropriately rather than wear jeans and T-shirts. As for running shoes... let's just say they are great for getting to work, but at work it's penny loafers or oxfords for the gentlemen and pumps for the ladies.

Naturally, common sense must prevail. If the job entails installing or moving equipment, physically handling items, dealing with fragile or soiled artifacts, and so on, the proper dress may be cotton pants and a smock. Similarly, some instructional roles – especially if they call for getting down on the floor with the kids – call for clothing that can take the occasional yank or encounter with paint.

Most information professionals may work in settings not requiring extensive physical exertion or exposure to dust or dirt. Such settings include editorial offices, libraries, newsrooms,

IT departments, and the like. Here, the influencing factors are closely associated with the organizational culture. A software startup may expect and encourage a casual style amenable to working through the night for the technical developers, but the sales team would likely be expected to project a more mainstream appearance.

What if it's unpredictable how the day will unfold? Where it is possible, it could be a good idea to keep something – say a blazer or a pair of 'perfect' shoes – stashed in the cubicle for those surprise moments when a client meeting is suddenly called!

Here is an ultra simple guide to appropriate dress in a Western or international work place. No attempt is made to address what would be appropriate in unique settings.

Tips on dress for everyone

These basics apply to all professionals and are based on commonly discussed principles. Naturally, certain industries and environments will have their own dress codes – the key is to be sensitive to the risk that others' opinion of your professionalism could be negatively impacted by your attire:

- If in doubt, go with the more formal of the options you are considering. There is little downside in being slightly overdressed and a lot of downside in being too casually dressed.

- Go with natural fabrics – wool, silk, cotton – and absolutely avoid polyester! (Microfibre is, however, acceptable in the case of women's suits.)

- Stick with quality: it is better to have three outfits or suits of high quality than to have six of lower quality. The lower-quality items quickly wear out and begin to look shabby; the high-quality items will stand the test of time as you keep the look fresh, for example with crisp shirts, ties, or scarves.

- Do not wear tight clothing that clings, bunches, gapes, or is otherwise revealing; clothes should *skim* the body.

- Avoid clothing with lettering and anything signaling affiliation with for example a political party or social cause.

- Invest in a color analysis to determine what colors look best given your skin tone and hair color. Be aware that skin tone and hair color will change as you age!

- No matter what, make sure everything you wear is in good repair and clean! It might seem superfluous and obvious, but just in case:

  - no scuffs on shoes and no worn heels

  - no kind of tear or rip or failure of hems and seams

  - no missing or broken buttons, buttons not firmly sewn to the garment, and no ripped button holes

  - no noticeable fraying or worn spots

  - no stains

  - no damaged or otherwise stressed handbags or briefcases.

- Bags: in front of clients, use the most expensive classic leather handbag or briefcase you can afford. Save up and get a good one – it will last your entire career if you take care of it. (Where the employer provides quality structured bags with the logo, such bags are appropriate.) More about bags below.

- No matter what, make sure your grooming is impeccable! These tips might seem superfluous and obvious, but just in case:

- Keep your hair clean, well cut, and above the collar, or at a maximum at shoulder level. (The 1960s and 1970s hippie days, when everyone had free-flowing hair, are *so* over – if you do want to have long hair, find a way to keep it neat and out of your face.)
- Nails must be perfectly cut. For men, nails must not extend beyond the finger. For women, nails extending more than a tiny bit beyond the finger require polish without chips. Really long nails (extending more than 3 millimeters past the finger) are not advised.

Dress guidelines for women

Less formal outfits	<ul><li>Slacks with a leather belt; cuffed shirt or formal blouse</li><li>Skirt with cuffed shirt or formal blouse</li><li>Shirt dress</li><li>Slacks with blazer or jacket</li><li>Flat shoes</li></ul>
More formal outfits	<ul><li>Skirt suit and shirt or turtleneck silk top</li><li>Slacks and shirt; shell dress with blazer or jacket</li><li>Shoes with heels (1–2 inches)</li></ul>
No-nos	<ul><li>Open-toed or sling-back shoes and sandals</li><li>Décolletage, bare midriff, spaghetti straps, shiny material, beads, or sequins</li><li>Flounces, frills, ruffles, and so on</li><li>Skirts above the knees</li><li>Bare legs – sorry ladies, you must wear stockings!</li><li>Vinyl fashion handbags 'du jour'</li></ul>
Colors	<ul><li>Go with colors that don't date: stick to neutral tones and use accessories or a jacket for impact – a grey, blue, or black base outfit can be accented by a colorful scarf or punched up by a vivid jacket</li></ul>

	■ Avoid stripes, checks, polka dots, and patterns unless they are extremely subtle – floral prints are not suitable except in a scarf
Tips	■ Coverage: 'The amount of skin you show is inversely proportional to the authority and expertise you will be perceived to have.' ■ Jewelry: wear few, conservative pieces (preferably silver, gold, or other 'naturals' such as amber, ivory, wood, coral, glass, and so on). Plastic does not cut it. ■ Makeup: keep it discreet. ■ Fashion: don't waste money on high-fashion clothing for work. Stick to pieces that don't associate with any given year. You can never go wrong with a classic jacket, a straight skirt, loose-fitting slacks, or a simple shirt.

Ulla's business 'uniform'

As I serve a variety of clients, I long ago chose a middle road. Often sitting in long meetings and on long plane rides, I refuse to suffer from uncomfortable clothing. I choose loose fitting styles and natural fabrics so that I can be comfortable no matter what.

In winter, I wear black dress slacks and shoes, a black turtleneck top (to feature a gold necklace), and a red or coral jacket. I always keep handy a pashmina shawl the same color as the jacket so that I may combine or switch the two – say, in a cold room or in a restaurant. My handbag or briefcase is black or red to match one of the colors I'm wearing.

In summer, I wear cream or light brown pants and turtleneck tops (to feature a multi-color pearl necklace) with a red or coral or brown–bronze jacket. My shoes are taupe or brown; the handbag or briefcase matches the jacket in color.

In addition to the necklaces mentioned above, I wear a simple gold bangle, a good watch, and two gold rings with a red stone. The jewelry is classy but not ostentatious.

No matter what the current fashion, the look is crisp and tidy and does not distract from what I have to say. I benefit from infinite combination possibilities as all my professional clothes and shoes fit into the winter and summer schemes.

Jill's business 'uniform'

When I worked in a corporation, I dressed in the preferred corporate attire for that era, which was dresses and skirts (and eventually dress pants). I tried to be a bit cosmopolitan in my style preferences, tending toward being more European. Since I love jewelry, I've always accessorized with necklaces and pins.

The turning point in my 'uniform' came when I became an independent information consultant. An attorney who worked as a consultant told me I would eventually select my clients by what I could wear. (Yes, you read that correctly.) Although that isn't exactly true, I have altered what I wear, tending more toward a comfortable professional attire.

First, I wear clogs all the time. I never knew that I liked clogs until I began working for myself. Clogs come in a wide variety of styles from casual to business, and I find them comfortable. If my feet aren't comfortable, then I'm not happy. Second, I always wear dress pants, a solid-color top, and either a jacket or an over-shirt. (I wish I could tell you the last time I wore a dress to a business function, but I can't.) Dress pants look nice, are comfortable, and are great no matter what I'm doing (flying, driving, giving a workshop, hauling equipment, and so on). My color coordinated outfits are accented with jewelry. I believe in well-made clothing and accessories in classic styles.

As a faculty member, my campus attire is quite different from my consulting attire. Faculty at my institution tend to wear business casual or casual attire most of the time, and I am no exception. When my faculty and consulting work intersect, I will dress in business attire recognizing that it is always better to over-dress for an occasion than to under-dress.

The most interesting attire choices occur when I attend a conference. Every conference has its own culture and it is important to know what attire is required. For example, when I attend the Special Libraries Association annual conference, I dress in business or business casual clothes, but may wear sneakers in order to keep my feet comfortable as I walk the often long distances to and between exhibit hall and conference center. In contrast, the Computers in Libraries conference is more casual and I've been known to wear jeans and a T-shirt on occasion. At the Venture Summit East event, where some of the attendees were venture capitalists, I wore business attire (with jackets and one-of-a-kind pieces of jewelry).

No matter the occasion, I want to fit in or dress better than those around me do. As I learned from a CEO many years ago, your attire can make a powerful statement about you. It can signify that you're 'one of the gang' – whether that means you are fitting in with CEOs or computer programmers. You want to use your attire to signal that you belong in a group. It can also signal that you are someone to be reckoned with or a person in a position of power. It is a lesson I've taken to heart, even though my feet are in clogs.

Dress guidelines for men

Less formal outfits	<ul><li>Slacks with leather belts</li><li>Cuffed shirts (or short sleeve shirts in hot climates) without a tie</li><li>Polo shirts (good quality)</li><li>Loafer style shoes</li></ul>
More formal outfits	<ul><li>Slacks with leather belts, blazer</li><li>Business suit – with tie in a solid color or conservative pattern</li><li>White shirts always look professional but colored or black shirts are appropriate; for example, a light blue shirt goes well with a navy blue jacket</li><li>Discreetly striped or textured shirts are acceptable</li><li>Oxford style shoes</li></ul>
No-nos	<ul><li>Sandals</li><li>Bare feet in shoes</li><li>Wrinkled anything</li><li>White socks (sock color should match the color of pants or shoes)</li></ul>
Colors	<ul><li>Go with colors that don't date but do not be afraid to be bold; for example, a salmon or aubergine colored polo shirt is perfectly appropriate in an informal setting.</li></ul>
Tips	<ul><li>Invest in perfect shirts: buy or have tailor make shirts for you that suit your neck and body shape and feel comfortable. Make sure to have on hand about two weeks' worth.</li></ul>

Tips on the appearance and contents of bags

You're perfectly attired for the presentation you are about to give or for the meeting you are about to attend. Don't ruin the image with a sloppy bag!

If work takes you out of the office, the bag you feature – and what's in it – is extremely important. You will need to have the right equipment on hand so you can be effective, yet you don't want to carry unnecessary bulk. Typically, we need to bring along a laptop or similar device, phone, a notebook or pad and pens for hand note taking, file folders with relevant documents, a wallet, and personal care items; however, consider the fact that the weather could call for an umbrella, and it may be desirable to carry a shawl in case a meeting room is excessively air conditioned. Water and snacks or a sandwich may be key items as well.

Options for types of bags are many, but the bag must be appropriate for the occasion, neat in appearance, and internally organized (you don't want lipsticks or bags of chips spilling out on the meeting table when you open your bag). Use pockets, organizers, and even zip-locked bags to keep bag contents neat and findable. Since it is easy to carry more than necessary, occasionally clean out your bag and reassess what is critical to have on hand. Don't be afraid to carry something that will help you stay looking professional, for example a travel-size lint brush if you are wearing clothes that attract lint and animal hair.

If your bag becomes worn, frayed, ripped, or stained, replace it.

For men

Men can never go wrong with a shoulder strap briefcase or document bag made of leather or good quality ballistic nylon. It is common to see professionals using such a bag with the employer's logo on it. Those needing to carry heavy equipment or lots of documentation are often seen using a wheeled bag.

For women

Women have a wider range of options. Some choose a handbag (sometimes called a purse) large enough to accommodate documents and a laptop; others use a dedicated computer or document bag and keep personal items in a smaller purse. Either way, the purse must be made of leather, unadorned except for clasps, and structured so that it stands up on its own ('sacks' are for the beach). In recent years, the marketplace has offered stylish wheeled 'detachables' allowing women the convenience of a rollerbag.

The evolution of Jill's bag

Over the years, what is in Jill's bag has changed. Rather than being on the road for a few hours, she may be on site with a client for an entire day. Her 'bag' has evolved from a leather zip-up portfolio in which she carried a three-hole punched pouch. In the pouch were items she knew she would need (paperclips, very small bottles of lotion, and hand sanitizer). She also carried extra pens and business cards in the portfolio and often a USB drive. Her cell phone, a constant companion, would be in her pocketbook. Now Jill carries a black over-the-shoulder multi-purpose bag containing everything she will need for the day including cell phone and charger, USB drive, umbrella, personal care items, glasses, client files, and so on. If necessary, her laptop and power cord also go into the bag. The bag zips closed so that she can keep her belongings safe. Outside pockets are great for any items she needs to access quickly like a subway pass. When on site, she may stash the bag in a coat closet and carry only the items she needs for a meeting.

About backpacks

Are backpacks acceptable? In some environments like university campuses and at some conferences, the backpack is ubiquitous and expected. If you are considering a backpack, first look at your work environment. What are the executives in your organization and your industry carrying? If you see backpacks used by those in positions superior to yours, then you can consider carrying one. If you don't see any, then consider a messenger bag or briefcase. If you are concerned about straining your back, review the available options for wheeled bags and select something that is appropriate and professional looking (brightly colored sports bags are not acceptable).

Tattoos, piercings, and purple hair: proceed with deliberation!

What if your brand includes 'body ornamentation' in the form of tattoos and the insertion of metal objects through noses, eyebrows, or cheeks? The growing popularity of such expressions of individuality has led to a common query: what types of such ornamentation are acceptable in the workplaces where we seek employment?

In our view, the key consideration here is long-term employability. Is it worth risking being rejected for a job many years in the future for the sake of expressing one's individuality now?

Understandably, managers hire with a view to the clients being served. Personally, a manager may not object to a nose ring or a tattoo, but he or she may be concerned how clients would react and may therefore – all else being equal – choose a candidate without self-inflicted features of appearance.

In every decade, the view of what is acceptable attire and adornment changes. Going back three hundred years, it was common for some men in Europe and North America to wear white powdered wigs. Earrings worn in pierced ears have been acceptable for some time for women and men alike. Now we are living in an era where multiple norms coexist, and that causes uncertainty. If you have – or are considering getting – tattoos, piercings, or any unnatural hair color, this section is for you!

It would be easy to tell you what to do – or not to do – but that would not cover every possible situation. Indeed, there are industries, organizations, and jobs where visible tattoos, body piercings, and unusual hair color (and style) will not limit your career advancement. There are, however, industries, organizations, and jobs where conforming to a specific norm is important. So what should you do?

First, look at the positions that interest you and at the types of organizations where such jobs exist. What are the norms there? Do photographs of executives and employees show people exhibiting creativity in dress, jewelry, and hair, or do they suggest a professional standard is being followed? They are important clues to an appearance likely to help get you hired.

Yes, some information professionals work in creative environments where people are encouraged to exhibit their personal style and where the latest fashion fads along with unusual hair color, tattoos, and piercings are seen as normal. Other information professionals work in environments that may not be avant-garde but still tolerate a wide range of styles, for example academic institutions. In workplaces where standing out from the crowd may be accepted, it will nevertheless be important to understand how your appearance could impact your career growth. Finally, some information professionals work in settings where mimicking the organizational norms is very important.

If you are interviewed for a job with an organization in which body ornamentation does not appear to be the norm, you may want to alter your appearance so that you conform to the standard dress code – for example, wear clothing that covers your tattoos and remove your piercings. If you hair is an unusual color or style, have it re-done. Yes, you are right in thinking the 'real you' is not showing up for the interview. However, removing distracting elements helps interviewers pay attention to your qualifications and interview answers as opposed to your appearance. During the interview process, pay attention to the organization's environment to determine what is truly deemed acceptable. If you receive a job offer and accept it, then you will need to decide how to reconcile the employer's expectations of your appearance with yours. Once in the position and comfortable with your new surroundings, you may then want to discuss with a trustworthy colleague whether you are at liberty to display your 'real you' at work.

Jill had a student who wondered if she should remove her nose ornament for a job interview at an academic institution located in a conservative area. Since the student's priority was to get the job, Jill's advice was to remove the piercing for the interview. Once the job was acquired, the student was able to assess the situation and decide if the piercing would be acceptable (it was).

If you are considering a change in your appearance, for example getting a tattoo, consider how it might be perceived by your current or future employers. We don't want to tell you to limit your self-expression, but we do want you to consider the possible consequences over the next five, ten, and 20 years (such as having your career path be shaped by your looks or having to wear long sleeves at all times). If the possible consequences are acceptable to you, then go ahead.

Finally, we should note that we know many tattooed and pierced information professionals who are climbing organizational ladders and making a difference in the profession. Some members of the profession with unusual hair color and haircuts are admired for their knowledge and professional contributions. We know professionals with an eclectic style of dress who are sought after as speakers and contributors. At some point in their careers, they all had to decide whether their appearance was likely to interfere with their career aspirations. Likely some became more conservative in appearance while they established themselves in the profession, then allowed their individual styles to emerge. Like them, keep in mind that a short-term compromise may be necessary in order to put yourself on a desired long-term path.

5

Looking for a job: tips and tricks

Going on a hunt

We all ignore conventional wisdom encouraging us to be looking for new opportunities at all times. If you are happy where you are, why bother? First, looking around for opportunities takes time you may not have – but what if a new opportunity presents itself today and you must respond immediately? Second, discovering new employment opportunities requires you to position yourself to be able to hear or see those opportunities. That means not only finding them once they are public, but also hearing about them before job announcements are sent out. In fact, you want people to think of you when they have an opening, and that occurs if you have been promoting your knowledge and skills – something that does not occur overnight. Finally, keeping a watchful eye on the changing job market will make you aware of the skills you need to acquire and give you time to build them.

Therefore, your job hunt must begin before you actually need to find a new position. We have all seen people who have lost their jobs and then are clueless about how to find a new one. These are people who have not been on a continuous hunt. When you hunt, you do reconnaissance first to discover where the 'big game' (jobs) are. You look for patterns, track marks, and other clues to help you understand the opportunities. You may have informal conversations with people, conduct web and database searches for additional information, and keep track of job announcements. If your time for reconnaissance is brief because you need to start your hunt immediately, you may want to hire a scout (placement firm) for assistance. A placement firm can work on your behalf to find potential opportunities; do be sure to read the contract carefully and understand who they are working for and how they are paid.

A good hunter keeps notes and you should too. Keep copies of interesting job announcements so you can track trends, discover what knowledge and skills you need to be able to offer, and understand who you need to include in your network so they will think of you next time there is an opening or opportunity. Note ideas about conferences you want to attend, presentations you want to give, or articles you should write in order to bolster your resume. Make a list of people you need in your network because they might help you find your next position, and then create a plan to meet them – in person or online.

After the reconnaissance, the hunter may stake out a particular area, knowing that she cannot cover every possible location where big game will appear. In our Web 2.0 world, it is easy to cover more territory with a job search, but you still need to focus. Not every job will be of interest, nor every environment, so narrowing your search – or even your reconnaissance activities – can help.

Conventional and unconventional hunting locations

We tend to look for a job the same way our parents did. First, we look at the most likely employers with defined jobs (and job titles) for people with our 'exact' skill set. We assume that if they already have people like us in their employment, then they will be predisposed to hire us. Although that is true, it means we have ignored other possible employers, including those not realizing they require our skills. In fact, some of the most rewarding positions might be with an organization in need of your core information skills in an area that may seem quite unusual to you, for example:

- sales
- training
- grant administration
- donor relations
- market research
- database design
- competitive intelligence
- content management.

Second, we look at job advertisements in newspapers and professional journals and send resumes to organizations we believe can use our skills. Although this strategy has worked in the past, many more people are now applying for fewer openings, so your resume may get stuck in a pile with many others. It is now critical to use other methods for finding job opportunities including networking (online and in person) and social tools. Using such alternate methods for finding opportunities will force you to market your skills and knowledge rather than your accomplishments. Keeping your eyes and ears open will undoubtedly lead you to opportunities that are different from what you had envisioned.

Networking is a powerful tool for finding opportunities, yet one we frequently do not do well. The ability to socialize for professional gain is a skill we all need to acquire. Like other skills, it must be practiced and used, or it will be lost. When can you network? When you:

- attend professional meetings, conferences, or workshops
- wait in the airport, stand on a subway platform, or ride on a bus
- volunteer in your community
- talk to customers or suppliers
- chat with friends at a party
- exercise at a fitness club.

Yes, networking can occur at any time and in any place. Although some settings are formal, most networking happens in informal ones. It is important to be ready to network no matter when it occurs. Here are some tips to help with your networking activities:

- Always have business cards on you, in a place you can reach quickly. Put business cards in whatever bag, briefcase, pocketbook, or wallet you carry.
- If you are going to a large event, carry 50–100 business cards to be sure not to run out.
- When you introduce yourself, clearly say your name and your organization's name or your area of interest. You can take 20–30 seconds for your introduction, which will go quickly. In order to make a smooth introduction, you should practice it. Jill used to practice her introduction in her car as she drove to networking events. She wanted her introduction – or infomercial – to be stated perfectly and to roll off her tongue effortlessly, but without making her sound like a robot.

- If people do not hear it correctly, say your name again. You want them to remember who you are.

- Exchanging business cards will help you remember a person's name and allow you to contact him or her afterwards. The other person also now has your contact information, which can be used to follow up with you or even make a referral.

- Although you are networking to advance your career, a successful networker makes the other person the center of the conversation. If you show interest in others, they will likely show interest in you. Along the way, you will learn more about those with whom you interact and build an authentic connection.

- Ask questions about what the person does, the event you are attending, or some topic you seem to have in common. Open ended questions are wonderful conversation starters.

- Conversations occurring during networking are generally not long. If you would like to turn a brief conversation into something much longer, or if someone wants to monopolize your time, ask if you can schedule a time to finish the conversation.

- Do not stand in one place at a networking event. Move around the room and approach people with whom you would like to talk. Challenge yourself to talk to four people who are each standing in different sections of the room.

- If you have trouble approaching people who are standing in groups, find someone who is standing alone and talk to him or her. The fact that an individual is standing by himself does not mean he isn't worth knowing.

- Be authentic. The real you – the genuine one – is an interesting person. There is no need to pretend to be someone you are not.

Some of the tips above will translate well to how you network online. In addition:

- Remember that your online network has no downtime. It is active even when you are not paying attention to it. Make sure to post online proper and professional information about you for the network to consult.

- Use a professional headshot of yourself in your social network profiles.

- Make sure photographs of you online are complimentary and positive. Photographs showing you in compromising and unflattering situations should never be online.

- Limit negativity. You do not want people to think of you as a sourpuss they don't want to be around.

- In every online social network, include information in your profile that says something about your knowledge, skills, and ability. Since the space is often limited, select your words wisely. Keep in mind that the online profile may be the first information someone receives about you.

Using bait to attract big game

The hunter may put out bait in order to attract game. In the same way, you may create a professional profile on social networking sites, place copies of your presentations and articles online, and develop a social media presence in order to attract job openings. In addition, you may use videos, blogs, podcasts, and real-time communication tools to attract opportunities. If possible, develop your own website (an online portfolio) containing information about you and linking to your materials (e.g. presentations). The site does not need to contain your resume, but should contain a well-written biography outlining your knowledge, skills, and professional contributions. Having a portfolio site does not suggest you are looking for a job, by the way. It does indicate your desire to develop a reputation outside of your current institution. If your institution allows you to create a portfolio on its website, you can do so, but you will have more flexibility if you create it on a website (domain) in your control.

The guidelines for letting prospective employers see your photograph online are not firm. For example, if you are late in your career, you may not want a prospective employer to see your gray hair. However, it has become so common for people to have their photographs on their online profiles and portfolios that not having a photo could make a hiring manager wonder why it is missing. As noted above, use a professional photo; a professional photographer will work with you to ensure you look your best, advise on what to wear (style and colors), and then capture you at the best angle in order to maximize your positives. After the photo shoot, you will be able to select the best one for your needs, and the photographer will make any final enhancements needed to perfect the image. Your photograph won't look like everyone else's because it was created especially for you.

Big game sighted!

One an opportunity is sighted, what do you need to keep in mind?

- Do your homework before you apply for a position. Research the organization and use what you learn to improve your communications with it. For example, are they embarking on a new initiative where you have specific knowledge and skills? During your interview, can you ask relevant questions to demonstrate that you understand the organization?

- Make sure the email address and phone number you use as part of your contact information are checked regularly. In addition, your email address should be professional ('speedracer@popularfreemailservice.com' is unlikely to provoke confidence in your professional skills) and your voice mail message should sound professional as opposed to being obviously meant for your friends.

- Most organizations accept cover letters, resumes, and applications electronically. Make sure your material looks good in digital form by using the portable document file (PDF) format whenever possible.

- Organizations want to hire good communicators. Make sure your cover letter and resume demonstrate that you are indeed a good communicator. Limit your use of jargon and eliminate typographical errors as well as grammar problems (see the specific resume tips in Chapter 6).

- Should you contact the organization and ask if your resume or application has been received? If you are truly interested in the position, you will want to be sure it has arrived. You might also want to show that you are very interested in the position by contacting the hiring manager. There is no one rule on what you can do, but there is a clear rule on what you don't want to do – you do not want to become a pest (no one wants to work with a pest). One phone call, phone message, or email to follow up politely is acceptable. The messages you want to convey to the hiring managers are:
  - you want to be sure your material arrived
  - they may contact you for more information
  - you are looking forward to meeting with them about the position in question.

- Prepare for any telephone or face-to-face interviews by engaging in mock interviews with trusted colleagues or your mentor. If possible, find a hiring manager to put you through a practice interview, since that person will ask more pointed and difficult questions. The more mock interviews you can do the better, because they will bring out questions you need practice answering and help you feel comfortable with the interview process.

- Practice any answers you are concerned about wording correctly. For example, if you need to have a very specific answer to a question such as why you left your last employer, then practice an answer until it becomes natural.

- After your interview, whether it is on the telephone or in person, send a thank you note to every person with whom you interacted. It is appropriate to send the note via email so that it is received quickly. Besides saying thanks, the formal note should reiterate why you are the best candidate for the job and indicate that you are awaiting the next step in the process. If any questions were left unanswered, it would be a good idea to include answers in the note ('After giving it some thought, I would like to add...').

Surviving the interview call

Many hiring processes now include a telephone interview where you are interviewed by one person or a committee. When all the applications have been reviewed and a group of top candidates identified, the telephone interview is used to select a smaller number of candidates – often three to five people – for on-site, face-to-face interviews. Your goal is to be one of those people, which means you must put your best effort forward during the telephone interview. Here are some survival tips:

- Ask the interview organizers ahead of time if they will tell you the names of those interviewing you, since it may be difficult to catch the names while on the call. Knowing their names enables you to address them personally to help make a more personal connection. If time allows, you could also do a little research on the committee members.

- Find a quiet place for the telephone interview. If you are at work, close your office door, go to a conference room, sit in your car, or find some other place where you will not be disturbed. You want to be heard clearly, and you want to be able to concentrate on the interview.

- A committee will use a speakerphone undoubtedly not yielding the best sound quality. If you cannot hear the interviewers clearly, tell them and ask them to repeat themselves if necessary. Do not be shy about doing this because you need to avoid misunderstanding questions.

- Have your resume, cover letter, and any other notes in front of you to help remember what the interviewers already know about you or and to help remind you of information you want to be sure to communicate correctly.

- Do not have anything in front of you that will distract you. If you are distracted, the interviewers will know it and surmise that you are not interested in the position.

- Sit in an attentive position and smile while you are on the call. Doing so will help you project a positive and 'can-do' attitude.

- Speak clearly and perhaps slightly more slowly than you usually do. You want the interviewers to hear your answers and understand them. Speaking too quickly may make it difficult for them to catch everything you are saying.

- Have a glass of water handy, since you will likely need a sip or two during the call. Coughing because your throat got dry is untoward.

- Always have questions to ask the committee, since you are also qualifying the members as potential future co-workers. If you do not have any questions, you may be seen as not being interested.

- At the end of the call, thank the committee members, remind them that they can contact you for more information, and tell them that you are looking forward to next steps in the process. That last part is important because it reinforces your belief that you are the best person for the position.

Who pays for the hunting road trip?

If you are traveling locally for a job interview, you should be prepared to absorb any travel costs including parking fees – they are part of your investment in the interview process. If it isn't obvious where you can park, ask your contact for advice. Should you be offered free parking, graciously accept it.

When getting to the job interview requires traveling long distance, the cost may be more than you are able to bear. Some organizations will cover the cost of travel, hotel, and food for a job candidate who must travel from a different region for the interview. You will need to decide if your desire for a position is such that you are willing to absorb any costs not reimbursed.

Hunters look for tracks (or what do your feet say?)

You have worked on your resume, purchased the perfect interview outfit, and practiced dozens of interview questions. You are trying to put forth 'the you' the organization will want to hire. Is that 'you' authentic? Is it the real you?

Walk into any group of people and look down at their feet. What do you see? Believe it or not, what people wear on their feet and the condition of those foot coverings can tell you much about them and may reveal their authentic selves. Comfortable, worn, well-maintained, damaged, new, classic, or latest-fad footwear all give clues, just as color and shape do. For example, a businessman from a technology company was at a conference in a very professional suit… and clogs, indicating he is someone who is comfortable making decisions that go against the norm and at ease with himself.

Now look at your shoes and consider what they say about you. Do they communicate the message you want to send? Everything you wear, all the words you write or speak, and everything about you that is available online (no matter where) are all communicating messages describing you. Is it all communicating the same message? Will potential employers see you as capable and confident, or are you sending mixed messages? If you are not sure, ask your mentor or trusted colleagues for their honest assessment.

Big game crossing

We have all heard of people who seemed to have the perfect job fall out of the sky in front of them when they weren't looking. What is not obvious is the work they did ahead of time in networking and becoming known in order to attract an opportunity. They likely had given presentations, written articles, and been a part of many conversations helping them become known and then seen as the best candidate for the position. Positioning oneself like that requires time and effort and does not occur instantaneously. If you follow the advice we are giving you in this book, you will have the presence and reputation to one day have the perfect job appear out of nowhere... and you will be ready for it.

We've been there

Jill and Ulla have been through all the job hunting problems, joys, and pains you are going through. We have had to hunt for jobs and we have had them land in our laps. Through it all, we remembered that looking for a job is a skill that everyone needs to perfect, so we have done our best to learn from our mistakes and the mistakes of others.

As Jill looks back at her job hunting experiences, one mistake standing out for her is using the standard cover letters she had at one point in time. She did not create truly customized letters for organizations she was approaching and now counsels others that the research in order to customize cover letters is an effort well invested to get the most positive impact.

Jill has had very few bad job hunting experiences, but she frequently shares the lessons she learned from one particular situation:

- Pay attention to what you see in people's offices when you go on site for an interview. For example, are the offices a mess? Is every desk covered in paper? Do people seem literally to live in their offices? Such signs could point to a culture where too much work is seen as normal, where the boss is too demanding, or where there is chronic understaffing. You could ask how many projects each person works on.

- The books on a person's bookcase can yield clues to what the organization values. Be sure to take a peek at the bookcase. You might ask, 'I notice that you have books on... How does that relate to the work you do?'

- If people can't answer common questions about the workday or office procedures, ask more questions. For example, if a person can't tell you when the workday starts, follow up with a question about what his or her workday is like. It could be that the culture of the organization has people working long hours overtime.

- Always do your research! Check the internet and any databases to which you have access for information about the organization. You may find useful clues to help you during the interview and to help you decide if the organization in question is a good fit for you.

Good fortune has been on Jill's side in the form of a number of positive job hunting coincidences. One of her favorite stories – as noted elsewhere in the book – is about two people who stopped in her office to ask directions as they tried to get to a meeting on time. During the quick conversation, one person asked, 'you have a Master's degree in library science, don't you?' When Jill responded 'yes', they said they would be back later. That quick exchange was the first step in a journey that led to Jill heading a new corporate library!

As Ulla looks back at her job hunting experiences, she notes that several jobs 'found her' because of the work she did outside her formal responsibilities. Being visible through speaking, writing, mentoring, and so on – as noted elsewhere in the book – she was a known quantity in the information industry when recruiters looked for talent. Anyone can emulate Ulla's career by beginning and continuing as she did: *give*. Give advice to students and colleagues, give content to newsletters, give speeches and seminars, give of yourself.

A certain amount of boldness was to Ulla's advantage when she reached out to a company to say 'you need to hire me because...'. The lesson here is that 'you never know': you never know whether an organization is in fact wondering about its options in the areas where you have expertise... so don't assume there is no opportunity simply because you don't see a job posting. Possibly the managers in the organization have never heard of skill sets like yours.

6

Creating your story: crafting a compelling resume

Every professional should possess – and keep up to date – a resume ready to be customized for any given job posting or organization. That's right... we tailor our resumes precisely to the role we are applying for or to a role we may be 'pitching' to a potential employer who has not yet realized he or she needs someone with our qualifications.

The resume may be the most important document you ever create. It needs a great deal of attention and effort on your part because it is a difficult task to distill professional and personal qualities and capabilities into a succinct capsule.

Fortunately, there are many resources to guide us. However, be warned: the advice you will find is likely to be conflicting as a result of the varying requirements in the public sector, academic environment, and private companies. We encourage you to take advantage of all the resources offered at the university you attend, in the local public library, or on the internet. Here are a few resources from the information profession:

- *The Info Pro's Survival Guide to Job Hunting* by Mary-Ellen Mort
  www.infotoday.com/searcher/jul02/mort.htm
- *Free Tools for Job Seekers* by Irene E. McDermott
  www.infotoday.com/searcher/jun09/McDermott.shtml

- Susan Ireland's resume site
  http://susanireland.com/resume/how-to-write/

The following brief overview is based on a seminar Ulla has been offering 'live' and on her website (*www.destricker.com/ pdf/CareerSeries1-REsumeRev3.pdf*). It walks step by step through the basic building blocks of typical resumes.

Print vs. online

Our focus here is the visual – printed or PDF – resume. When a job posting calls for submission online, you must follow different guidelines. A key contrast is that while we strive for a concise visual resume, the electronic version may contain lots of detail to enhance the likelihood of being found by a search engine. You may not know whether the system into which you submit an e-resume is keyword searchable at the employer's end, but because there are no format considerations, you may safely provide much more detail than you would in a standard visual resume (for example, listing every software tool with which you have worked). It is highly recommended that you prepare blocks of text ready to upload into the likely categories presented by an online resume submission system.

Resume as sales instrument

As a capsule of professional essence, a resume is primarily a sales instrument. You are not required to account for everything you have done in your life. The sales tool highlights those aspects of your professional offerings most likely to engage the reader – that's why we need to create tailored versions for every job application. Each submission should be tuned to what we believe will get the particular employer's attention. And there's an immediate challenge: we are not the ideal authors of our own resumes because we often are blind to our own strengths. Someone who had worked as activities coordinator was at first puzzled when Ulla said, 'you must be highly effective as a multitasker'... but then realized that indeed, that work experience could be translated into a skill applicable to many positions in the information profession. Similarly, Ulla was amazed when someone said, 'eight years of running an import–export business can't be relevant'. Of course business experience is relevant – one need only think of aspects such as client relations, attention to detail, budget and logistics planning, and so on. In an ideal world, your resume would be crafted by a trusted colleague who knows you well – and that would be wishful thinking! However, once you are done writing, you do want to show your drafts to trusted colleagues and friends, asking for their honest reactions about the content (do you recognize me?) and about the appearance (does it look crisp and professional and would you be motivated to read it, based on how it's laid out?).

Three common myths: don't believe them!

Myth 1

A resume must be two pages only. There are exceptions – academic and government settings, for example, tend to require much more detail than is the case in the private sector. Our recommendation is to stick to the two-page format with an appendix containing additional detail – such as publications or speeches. Be sure to refer to any appendix in the two-page resume proper – say, for example, 'additional information in the appendix' in square brackets at the bottom of a list. The bottom line: better to go to three easily readable pages than to crowd information onto two pages that are difficult to read. The overriding concern is the convenience and reading experience of the reader.

Myth 2

Hide awkward information such as gaps in employment. Our view is that it's better to put everything out... than to give an employer the opportunity to find information you did not provide. Account for any employment gaps. It is legitimate to put 'raised a family' or 'traveled' as entries in a sequence of jobs. If you have long experience, it is legitimate to summarize it ('prior to [year], held several positions in...') so as to draw the reader's attention to more recent information. The cover letter is a good place to mention how any 'unusual' activity in your life contributed to your professional growth or suitability for a job.

Myth 3

We must account for our personal interests in resumes. Absolutely not. No employer will be impressed to read that your interests include travel, reading, and knitting. What we *can do* is feature personal pursuits with relevance for the job we are applying for. Volunteer activities are a rich source for shining a light on the skills developed in the course of our service. For example, if you organized a community event, you can credibly say 'gained management skills organizing the annual fund raiser involving attendees from 12 surrounding towns' or 'gained meeting management skills through serving on the board of directors for the local branch of the Red Cross'.

Essential sections in a resume

There are five essential sections in a resume, not including references: tag line, key features, your experience, your education, and 'everything else'. What about references? It is standard to state 'References available on request' but, if you have permission, why not just list the references right then and there to save the reader the effort of obtaining the contact information from you?

Section 1 Tag line

Your tag line is the four- to seven-word distillation of who you are as a professional. It is similar to a slogan in its brevity and evocativeness. Its purpose is to convey instantly to the resume reader what kind of professional you are. As an illustration, back when I worked at Micromedia in Toronto – it was later sold to ProQuest – I commented to its founder that although the name Micromedia was well chosen for the original microfilm products, it no longer adequately described the many publishing ventures of the company. I then suggested the tag line 'Canada's Information People' – and I still have the mug. Let me further illustrate by saying that my esteemed colleague Cabot Yu, who puts on many events for information professionals in Canada, could have a tag line 'pioneering and entrepreneurial organizer of professional events' and my own tag line could be 'knowledge management expert' as well as 'energetic spokesperson for associations for information professionals'. Spend the time it takes to come up with a tag line you feel captures your essence and rings true – and pair up with colleagues to trade ideas. Here are some examples of tag lines:

- recent graduate with strong web skills
- experienced special library manager
- library systems expert with experience in large scale systems
- public library change-agent manager.

Section 2 Key offerings

The body of the first page of the resume consists of bullet points – or a brief statement – showing what your main offerings are. It's helpful to provide at least two groups of bullets or two statements to separate professional qualifications from personal abilities. (Consider the personal segment of the key features your opportunity to signal to the reader what it's like to work with you.) Here are some examples.

Example 1

Special library operations and management:

- experience with client needs assessments and strategic planning
- documented positive impact on knowledge workers' productivity
- demonstrated success in vendor negotiations and budget management.

Client relations and team building:

- track record in building strong, positive client relations and aligning service priorities with client goals
- innovator with achievements in coaching teams and staff members.

Here is a special librarian featuring a track record in management and emphasizing skills in client relations and team building. He or she is essentially saying to the reader 'you need to hire me because I know how to find out what knowledge workers need, deliver it to them, and thus enhance their productivity.' Pay attention to the use of terms such as 'documented', 'demonstrated', and 'track record' – in other words, these are not just claims, there is evidence.

Example 2

Public library operations and management:

- extensive experience managing larger public libraries in mixed-demographic areas
- track record of productive trustee relations
- demonstrated success in developing programs aligned with user groups' needs.

Marketing and funding:

- significant achievements in boosting library visibility and traffic (in-person and virtual)
- strong networking skills applied to building effective support in the community.

A public library manager features the accomplishments and skills that would likely resonate with trustees. The job posting or the location of the branch likely indicated that experience with a mixed demographic would be relevant. Of course, the first challenge for public libraries is funding so that aspect is given its own set of bullets.

Example 3

Technical skills:

- accomplished web and systems professional (15 years)
- track record of delivering projects on time and on budget.

Interpersonal skills:

- experience in multicultural settings
- strong rapport building skills to facilitate team work.

In this example, interpersonal skills are featured, and it is a good idea to include such personal characteristics if the position being applied for is likely to require them. If you take a moment to consider the question 'what are some of the traits people have often complimented me on' you may arrive at phrases such as 'passionate researcher' or 'tenacious problem solver'.

In the context of the key features, how much detail should be included on the tools, systems, or databases with which we are familiar? Be specific if the job posting called for it, but avoid listing software skills that are generally taken for granted. By all means showcase exceptional skills if they are relevant. There are some typical phrases to avoid, however:

- 'strong communication skills'
- 'superior organization skills'
- 'excellent team player'.

Why? Because such phrases could mean anything and therefore mean nothing, so they are a waste of space. Test your proposed phrases by asking:

- Would this phrase appear on 90% of resumes?
- What's the proof I have that skill?

Section 3 Professional experience – chronological or functional

The segment on work history may be the longest unless your experience is brief. Here, we document where we acquired the skills and accomplished the successes shown in the key features. The structure of the information is standard – we state where we worked and in what function, then list our achievements (not just our duties).

A chronological listing is straightforward, and it is what every university career counselor tells students to construct. Although it can be perfect for someone whose career has progressed in order, it doesn't work for someone who has had multiple careers or who wants to switch careers. Some advisors therefore suggest a functional arrangement where all the employer names are grouped together and all the functions are grouped together. That could be a workaround if you believe your experience isn't as balanced or progressive as you would like.

The key concern here is the message sent by the information. We want to stress how we made an impact, not repeat a job description. That said, some jobs are predominantly operational in nature, particularly ones we may hold as interns; look for the 'what was different when I left' angle.

Brevity is always a virtue – remember how our goal is to make it easy for the reader to take in the information we want to convey. Strive to avoid stating the obvious and concentrate on the messages that might resonate with the reader. If it's possible, a bullet for each job to indicate the major learning would signal to the reader that you pay attention and keep adding to your skills.

Section 4 Education: academic and ongoing

We are now, of course, on page 2 or possibly page 3. The reader assumes we have or are completing the MLIS degree; where it was or is obtained is of less interest. Some argue, on the other hand, that certain universities are so prestigious they should be mentioned. I would handle such a situation by putting prestigious institutions in the Key Features bullets – for example, 'Undergraduate degree in economics from Harvard'.

Those who are students or who have little work experience often ask whether to list courses taken while in graduate school. Naturally, the context of the position being applied for is your guide here, and certainly if you undertook significant project work as part of a course, that would be relevant information. However, in general, listing graduate school courses is discouraged.

Ongoing education belongs in the fourth segment as well – it's good to signal to the reader how we keep up with developments and grow as professionals. If you take a lot of shorter seminars, that fact can be generically described without appending a long list.

Section 5 'The goodie bag'

Here we feature volunteer work, association activities, awards, and anything else not already covered. The title of the section could be something like 'Professional activities and volunteer work'; its purpose is to show your engagement in your profession and in the community. The information presented here rounds out the picture being formed in the reader's mind about what value you bring to the table.

Accuracy, consistency, and economy of words

The mantra here is 'the care you take with your resume is an indicator of the care you take on the job'.

First, be sure to give your resume draft to multiple critiquers and proofreaders who can spot the errors you can't. It is virtually impossible to proofread one's own work, so you may wish to trade services with colleagues. Keep in mind that a single error may be sufficient to get your resume rejected; readers will instinctively sense the correlation between the quality of the resume and the likely quality of your work.

Though not as serious as outright errors, inconsistency can make the reading experience more difficult than necessary. For instance, pick a style for dates ('December 2009 to October 2010' vs. '12/09–10/10') and stick to it. Be alert to the fact that word processing programs sometimes convert a simple hyphen into a long dash, and avoid ambiguities such as '08/09' where the meaning could be August 2009 or September 2008.

Be consistent in your choice of nouns or verbs. Most people find verbs more active and therefore prefer them, but it's your call so long as you stick to the style you chose ('coordinated' vs. 'coordination of').

Get out a vacuum and ensure there are no unnecessary words anywhere. For example, the word 'both' adds no new or useful information in the statement 'served both faculty and students'; 'served faculty and students' is perfectly clear.

Finally, avoid redundant geography. If it is likely to be obvious to readers where something took place, we don't need to state it. 'University of Toronto' and 'University of Copenhagen' require no further information as to the location. Conversely, academic institutions not likely to be known by resume readers should be geographically placed.

Visual appearance

The immediate impression a reader forms based on visual appearance matters more than you may believe. A few key pointers:

- The text should be easily readable by potential employers wearing glasses. If you use Tahoma or Calibri font – examples of modern looking, easy-to-read fonts – size 11 (or 10.5 for bullet lists) is good.

- Your address information should occupy a single line under your name and tag line, in 9 point font. The information must be present, but what could possibly be less interesting to the reader than where you live?

- Be unafraid to use color and graphic elements to give the resume class and visual appeal. You need the reader to think instantly 'oh, this looks great' and start reading in an impressed frame of mind. With credit to Ford, job 1 is to grab attention; job 2 is to show you deserve it.

Here is, unfortunately, an example of many resumes' first page. Bland in appearance, it spends valuable real estate on address and degree information, facts telling the reader nothing about why the applicant warrants attention. By halfway down the first page, the potential employer has no clue what the applicant has to offer.

Firstname Lastname

Address information
in type size equivalent to all the rest of the resume
occupying multiple lines
even using 'Tel' and 'Email' in front of obvious phone
number and email information

EDUCATION
Degrees and universities

Below are sample illustrations of the first page of more appropriately formatted resumes to show how key information is featured 'up top' and how a modern, clean appearance aids reading.

All names, addresses, institutions, work functions, and dates are fictional. The colors (blue, mauve, green) used for names and headers in the original examples could not be replicated in this book.

Example 1: Joan's resume is fairly conservative, yet easy on the eye. Notice how much white space there is.

JOAN SHANNON, MIS

Experienced Special Library Manager

123 Oak Road Northtown, Ontario M5N 3W7 jshannon88@rogers.com 416-123-4567

Professional Profile:

- Experience since 2001 in special libraries managing research, reference, and licenses
- Proven ability to develop and maintain excellent client relationships through outstanding customer service
- Demonstrated success in meeting extremely tight deadlines serving demanding clients
- Highly effective team leader, known for long-term staff retention through the creation of a supportive and collaborative team environment

Employment History:

Manager, Library Services, 2006–present: **Metro Insurance, Toronto**

- Transformed library into proactive and outreach focused partner for business teams
- Developed project-start service model in collaboration with team leaders
- Pioneered use of wikis to capture subject matter expertise

Information Specialist, 2001–2006: **City Financial, Montreal**

- Bullet describing specific accomplishments and areas of responsibility
- Bullet describing specific accomplishments and areas of responsibility
- Bullet describing specific accomplishments and areas of responsibility

Example 2: Gretchen goes a little further by using color for her name and headings.

Gretchen Cory, MLS

567 Morley Road London, UK B27 6SE g.cory@gmail.com 44-1753-274403

Sales & Marketing Professional, Corporate Markets

Profile

- Successful, achievement oriented information professional with a proven track record delivering consistently over-quota sales results
- Consistent delivery of team results based on leadership and management skills
- Appreciated by customers as a dedicated, proactive consultative resource with specific expertise in their information related challenges

Business Experience

Tripps Publishing London UK April 2004 – Present

VP, Sales and Marketing

- Built dedicated sales team and launched new product line nationally
- Set up and managed product development client advisory group
- Met or exceeded sales target every year since 2005

Legal Times Cambridge UK January 1997 – April 2004

National Director, Corporate Accounts (02–04)

- Bullet reflecting specific achievements
- Bullet reflecting specific achievements

Marketing Manager (99–02)

- Bullet reflecting specific achievements
- Bullet reflecting specific achievements

Product Specialist (97–99)

- Bullet reflecting specific achievements
- Bullet reflecting specific achievements

Example 3: David uses tables to set off his key feature statement and to organize his professional experience information. Notice how the tables harness the dates and keep them in their place. (Unless you use such a device, do not "slop" date information to the right hand side, forcing the reader's eye to jump across the page.)

DAVID DJURS 11 Neelsgade 2TV, 2100 Copenhagen ddjurs@hotmail.com +45 56 78 90 12

Information Professional with Significant IT Experience

HIGHLIGHTS

- Masters Degree Equivalent in Information Science
- Integrate quickly with new organizations and teams
- Experience with Open Source Software and Tools
- Multilingual (Spanish, Danish, English)

EMPLOYMENT HISTORY

Regional Schools Directorate, Copenhagen DK	2008–
Intranet Manager • Full responsibility for design and development of content rich intranet to support curriculum development and testing • In charge of training for over 10,000 teachers	

OTHER EXPERIENCE

Municipal Government, Aalborg DK	2006–7
Intern • Implemented open source search software for public works database • Provided IT support to front line personnel	

EDUCATION

Information and Library Technologies Masters Degree Equivalent University of Copenhagen	2006
Bachelor's Degree, Business and Finance University of Barcelona	2004

VOLUNTEER WORK

Local School Boards, Spain and Denmark Tutor/Advisor • Set up tutoring programs in collaboration with parents and teachers • Developed progressive series of courses in IT skills for secondary school students	2002–

Example 4: Alice decides to depart from the standard style and right justify her text. Again, the table format keeps everything neatly organized.

111 Harner St Toronto, ON M5S 3L1 (647) 304-2202 alicekuna@hotmail.com	# Alice Kuna, MLIS

Recent graduate – Exceptional Programming Skills – Russian Speaker

Summary of Skills

• Software Applications: Names of applications • Programming: Names of programs • Operating Systems: Names of operating systems	Technical
• Educated in the UK – understanding of multicultural matters • Undergraduate degree and MLIS in Canada	Multicultural
• Ability to grasp complex detail quickly • Successful in creating positive, productive team dynamics • Dedicated to project success no matter what it takes	Personal

Programming Projects

Web-Based Russian-Language Music Training Tool [dates]
• Built an interactive website teaching music to Russian speaking children
• Designed instructional exercises using XXX

E-commerce [dates]
• Built an online health supplements store
• Created interface using XXX
• Used XXX to support e-commerce

Sports League Website [dates]
• Created website interface using XXX and XXX
• Used XXX to manage calendars, schedules, and transportation logistics

The cover letter

If the resume is a challenge, the cover letter is truly a formidable task!

Repeat the name, tag line, and address information from the resume to tie the two together.

Take advantage of the fact that the cover letter is your opportunity to *have a voice*. Make the text as vivid and lively as possible, and focus on explaining why you are the ideal hire. Speak to the specifics of the job posting and add information you believe might set you apart from others. Should you have had the privilege of working with a well-known individual, someone the reader is likely to recognize, by all means drop the name (with permission of course).

It is essential for the reader to get the impression the cover letter was written specifically for the application in question. Avoid *like the plague* a cover letter that is so general it could be submitted for every job you seek. As with the resume itself, seek help from colleagues and ask for ruthless critiques.

Here is an example of a cover letter with 'voice'. The candidate is applying for a senior strategic communications role – but the tone and progress of the letter can be used in any application:

I am the ideal candidate for the position of XXX at [employer]. My qualifications are extraordinarily applicable to what [employer] needs to develop and drive its strategic agenda.

In the positions I have held, there has been a consistent need for strategic and political savvy and relationship management expertise. My natural inclination to big-picture thinking and long-term strategic visions led me to use sophisticated communications skills throughout to engage others, often in challenging environments:

- Working at [types or names of organizations], I have developed a keen sense of political finesse and communications nuance. The elements of stakeholder communications for influence and results are by now instinctual in my work.
- My career experience has given me extensive insight into good governance and committee management.
- In particular, I am adept at leadership through credibility and relationship management. I am highly skilled in building rapport with team members, stakeholders, collaborators, and clients.

My key career accomplishments substantiate that I possess the experience required for the position:

- At [past employer], I set up and managed the strategic management and employee recruitment section, in which role I developed and implemented...
- At [past employer], I developed and implemented policies and guidelines for the application and use of an electronic network and a database to collect relevant information on activities and budgets related to...
- At [past employer], I led the evaluation of... and achieved success in image, branding, and harmonization initiatives.

My practical insight, in-depth knowledge of management and communications practices, and natural instinct for strategic positioning and vision will enable me to have a strong positive impact on [employer] in the development and leadership of its strategic agenda. I look forward to working with the management team at [employer] to realize its goals for driving research and innovation.

I thrive in a dynamic and vision inspired environment and I am ready to put all my experience and talent to work for [employer].

7

Knowing where you want to go: plan... but let chance have a chance!

Getting an honest career assessment

Sometimes people get a career idea in their heads and then pursue the idea without understanding if it is right for them. Although a career counselor could put you through an assessment tool meant to tell you what areas would be best for you, a cheaper – and perhaps more effective – assessment can be made by asking your friends and colleagues the type of work they think you should be doing. Thinking about questions like 'what five jobs do you think fit my skills and personality?' can give you ideas and perhaps start interesting conversations. Ask five to ten of your friends or work colleagues, then look for similarities in the answers. Often our friends know us better than we know ourselves and make good suggestions. Although you may not make an important career decision based on such input, it should give you information that is worth considering – especially if your career idea is the exact opposite of their suggestions.

As a child, you are always being asked what you want to do when you grow up. Even as adults, we continue to think about what we want to do 'when we grow up' as if we are not yet doing what we were meant to do. The questions allude to the fact that we are supposed to plan our careers and our futures. The truth is that we often leave our careers to chance, as if we don't care about what happens.

It is unrealistic to ask a child to plan her career. Even university students are still exploring their options and may not be ready to say 'this is really what I want to do'. In fact, it is common for a university student to change her mind several times during a four-year degree program. Once graduated, it is expected that she will settle down into a specific career path; yet it is now normal to have several different careers during a lifetime. If you haven't decided on a career or have changed your mind a few times, you are not alone.

However, in order to be successful in any career, you need to have a plan.

A plan helps to move you toward your goal. If you intend to work in a specific type of organization, then your plan will include the steps needed to make you desirable to such organizations, ensure that you are known by the right people, and get the necessary experiences. Your plan becomes your road map. Like any road map, it contains directions, mileage (assessments), and markers (to ensure that you're on the correct path). Before you create your career road map, prepare.

Getting ready for the trip

Before you create a road map, you need to decide the direction you want to take your career. Are you interested in a specific type of work? Do you want to work for a certain kind of organization? Is a specific passion propelling you? Although there are many tests to help you decide where your skills and interests lie, the easiest thing for you to do is to pay attention to your likes, dislikes, curiosities, and so on. You may want to keep a journal where you chronicle your career interests, including descriptions of jobs and courses that excite you.

Having an idea – or many ideas – of what you want to do will help you plan your course of action. Just as on a road trip, once you have a destination in mind, you can begin to plan how to get there:

- What knowledge and skills will you need for your career? Can you acquire them through coursework, on the job training, or how else?
- Who should be in your network to help you make connections to people in a position to hire you?
- With whom should you interact online via the social media sites?
- What conferences do you need to attend?
- Where should you try to get published?

Notice that thinking about the questions above is meant to put you in control of your career. Gone are the days when you can leave your career to chance. Many search for opportunities, and it benefits you to be as prepared as possible in order to be the preferred candidate for a job or the person tapped by a headhunter.

Some people have no idea what direction they want to go in. For them, there are endless possibilities ahead and all of them are interesting (or maybe none of them are interesting). The wealth or dearth of possibilities stops them from creating even a draft of a career path. If you are among those who do not know which direction to take, understand that making a decision can be liberating and crucial for your future success. The liberation comes from being able to learn first hand what you really like or don't like. If you decide a given job is not what you want, then you can better define your next direction. Although conventional wisdom has been that you should stay in a job for two years before moving on, staying for a shorter period of time may be appropriate as long as you can explain the reasons to a future employer. If you take a job and realize you truly dislike it, it is acceptable to leave and look for something else.

Taking a detour... or two

Jill became attracted to libraries in elementary school (fifth grade). She began working in libraries and continued while working on her undergraduate degree. However, she then became interested in working in radio and took a detour for a couple of years after graduation. The detour gave her a chance to rest before heading to graduate school and allowed her to pay some bills – but it gets better: being a part-time announcer helped her to become a more confident public speaker, and her work elsewhere in the organization gave her an understanding of the news media and advertising. After such experiences, Jill moved on to get a Master's degree and took another five year detour working in information technology (IT). IT touches everything we do, so being a programmer-analyst and working with a variety of systems gave her knowledge she deems irreplaceable.

At the time, Jill's time in radio seemed totally unrelated to what she wanted to do. In hindsight, she recognizes what she learned from it and how it relates to her work now. She was lucky. Detours can pull a person off-course, so it is important to understand why you are taking one and what you will gain from it.

You may find yourself taking a career detour for a number of reasons, such as the need to take an offer in order to ensure that you have income. When you do, keep a watchful eye for learning in the job that may contribute toward your real career goal. Perhaps you can demonstrate an ability to handle increased responsibility, improve communication or computer skills, or develop important contacts. Whatever it is, make sure you can explain those benefits to others, feature them in your resume, and highlight them during future job interviews. A potential employer may be thrilled with your detour if its benefit is clear.

Watch out for rough roads ahead – but use them to your advantage

No matter how well you research a potential employer, you may find yourself working in less than desirable conditions. Rough stretches of road are survivable and they can provide useful learning opportunities and great networking.

First, let us think about how to avoid rough patches. You must research your potential employer as thoroughly as possible. You are going to spend at least eight hours a day with the employer – more waking hours each day than you will spend with your family and friends – so you need to know if the environment will be a good fit for you. Check newspaper and financial databases for information on the organization and, if possible, check legal databases for any recent legal trouble. Use social media sites to find information on current and past employees and see what they might be saying about the organization. If you know any people who have worked for the organization, contact them and ask for any input they can offer about the organization's environment. Be sure to frame your questions in a positive way, asking if there is something you should know about the organization that is not generally known. Doing so provides an opportunity for your contact to volunteer additional information.

When you interview with people in the organization, be sure to ask open ended questions such as 'what do you like about the work environment?' Pay attention to the demeanor of employees you meet or pass in the hallway. Do they seem genuinely happy? If they seem stressed, you could look for a chance to ask a question about the stress level of the environment. Look at the physical environment: what do the offices look like? An office reflects what a person and an organization value, so it can be a good clue how the workplace functions. Is the office space comfortable? Is every office too cramped? Does the recruiter say the organization is top notch while the space tells you otherwise? Does the interior decorating indicate a strict hierarchy or egalitarianism?

Regardless of all those impressions, even if the environment does not seem perfect, you may have bills to pay and need to take the job. In that case, consider this a detour in your career path. Use it as a learning experience, which can help you stay positive, and remain alert for other opportunities.

If you did take the job – how do you survive an untoward environment?

Remember that you will not be in any environment forever. If the environment is extremely caustic, you may decide to leave in a matter of weeks or months. You may also find that staying longer could provide some benefits; for example, you could be working on a great project in a lousy environment. Keep these ideas in mind:

- Understand clearly what the benefits of your position are. Write them down and keep them handy for those times when you need to remind yourself that benefits should outweigh negatives. When the negatives outweigh the benefits, it is time to plan on making a move to a different organization.

- Because it is a great project – one that could lead to something even better with your next employer – you may decide to stay until the project is completed.

- Know that you are not alone. It is possible there are others who feel the same way you do. It may take time to find colleagues on your wavelength and then to feel comfortable sharing survival tactics, but once you find those colleagues, they are likely a good work support network. Keep a positive attitude and avoid being viewed as a whiner – you don't want your next employer to hear stories about how you always complained while you were at work.

- Network. Whether it is through meetings, conferences, virtual conferences, email, or social media, you will need to network with as many people as possible to give you a larger support network and to help you make the connections for finding your next job.

- Ensure your reputation is distinct from that of your organization. When people think of you as a professional, they should think of you and not of your organization (especially if your organization is viewed negatively for whatever reason). Give conference presentations, write articles, and create a professional profile for yourself in some of the online social networks. Make sure professional peers and potential employers can find positive and flattering information about you and your work. Building a reputation takes years, so start work on it early in your career and then maintain it. (As an aside: if your organization does not want you giving presentations, writing articles, or blogging, then you will need to find other avenues for making yourself known. You might get involved through social media with other like-minded professionals to share tips and techniques informally, with the aim of positioning yourself as an expert.)

- Invest in conferences and other professional events – that is, invest in yourself. Many organizations limit funds for attending workshops and conferences, but even if you are on a limited budget you must invest in yourself and find ways of attending workshops and conferences (in person or online). Yes, you may have to use your vacation time and your own money to grow your opportunities. If you want a rewarding and satisfying future, you should see the investment in conferences as being worth it. There are ways to rein in costs – always look for opportunities like sharing a room or transportation, staying with a friend, volunteering to help with arrangements in exchange for a fee discount, and so on.

Arriving at your destination

Your first destination on your road trip is a great job in your field of interest. Undoubtedly, it will be followed by other jobs, ones we hope are personally and professionally fulfilling.

However, as you progress in your career, keep in mind that your work is a means to an end. It is a means to living comfortably. It is a means to making a difference in the lives of others or in your industry. It is also the means – the path – to a time when you will retire. Although having a wonderful career is important, being retired is the goal at the end of the road. Are you doing something you like and can do until you stop working? Are you building skills and interests to stand you in good stead in your retirement years? Are you building savings (a nest egg)? Those are all important questions to ask yourself from time to time. You may find that keeping your eye on what you are ultimately trying to do may help you focus, get you through a rough patch, and create the life you want.

The pivot

Entrepreneurs who start businesses often find that their business idea is not panning out. For example, one may have an idea for a new social media tool, and then discover that the idea is a bad one. Rather than abandoning everything, the entrepreneur will pivot (change direction), use what has been learned, and embark on a new idea. Among entrepreneurs, the pivot is not a sign of failure but rather a sign of understanding more about their capabilities and the market.

We often seem intolerant of people who change their minds about their careers, yet we have all known someone who made a major, successful shift in his or her career path. If you decide that you need a major shift, do not be afraid to make it. If you have given it forethought, considered the pros and cons, understand the risk, and created a new road map, then do it! You may have just put yourself on the road to career success you were meant to follow.

Navigating organizational culture: understanding politics

No matter what type of organization you work in, you will be faced with a culture to learn and navigate. Sadly, we do not take classes on how to survive and thrive in organizations. Learning is often carried out through trial and error, and it can be fraught with frustration. During that trial and error, you could easily make a regrettable slip in conduct. With that in mind, let's offer some keys for success.

Become familiar with the organizational structure and culture

We might say that in any organization, every person has his or her place. Indeed, every employee fits into a defined organizational structure that goes from the top of the organization (for example president, chairperson, chancellor, dean) to the bottom. The structure communicates formal power and responsibilities. The higher up in the organization a person is, the greater his or her responsibilities and power. In most organizations, the job title will provide clues as to organizational rank.

Where does your department report, and in turn where does the larger unit fit? How close are you to the top of the organization? The answers to those questions will assist you in understanding your position in the organization and your sphere of influence. If you seem to be at the bottom of the organization, do not despair at your lack of influence; in time you can promoted up the organizational ladder and become more influential.

You do not need to memorize the organizational structure, but you should be very familiar with it. Be sure that you can recognize your superiors and can articulate what they do. Know who the other people are at the level of your boss and how they relate (or interact) with your boss. Understand if your boss is in an influential position among her peers or if she is at a disadvantage (and why). Investigate your internal clients' responsibilities and challenges. The more you understand about your clients, the better you'll be able to meet their needs and delight them with your products and services.

It is important to understand an organization's *informal* structure and culture. It is expressed when you see:

- who is relied on for information and advice
- who gets consulted about important decisions
- whose opinions are held in higher regard
- who knows organizational news first
- who has the organizational leaders' trust.

You need time and patience to discover this structure. Although colleagues may be willing to point out pieces of it, it is unlikely anyone will be in a position to describe it in detail – partly because some elements of it are not supposed to be obvious. Rely on your eyes and ears, and once you have an idea about the structure, tap into it to test ideas and gather information. Use it respectfully and carefully so that it remains available to you – abusing the informal structure quickly leads to being shut out of accessing it.

The organizational culture, like the structure, is informal yet extremely powerful. Ulla defines organizational culture as the sum total of the behaviors being accepted and rewarded – quite apart from any formal vision and mission statements framed on the wall. It has been said that 'culture trumps strategy', and we agree that regardless of what any CEO pronounces, the culture of the organization determines what gets done day in and day out. As a simple example, a culture that accepts tardiness at meetings results in more and more tardiness, in effect showing disrespect for employees who have the courtesy to be on time (never mind the cost of the lost productivity). A culture accepting smokers taking double the amount of break time non-smokers take is in effect rewarding employees who don't pull their weight, and the non-smokers may resent the unspoken inequality. A culture demanding no particular rigor in documenting the sources of ideas or recommendations may evolve into a culture where opinion drives policy and decision making – an environment posing challenges for information professionals who innately emphasize professionalism in backing up suggestions or advice!

Gain political power

Most people disdain the use of strategy to obtain a position of power whether in connection with a resource, project, or job. We often use the phrase 'playing politics' because we see it as a game with winners and losers. In reality, we want to create win–win situations where each side sees a benefit. Therefore, politics is a way of understanding and using the power that exists in the organization in order to create organizational success.

How do you gain political power? First, you need to do your job well. You must be seen as someone who wants to ensure the organization benefits from your knowledge and skills; you will have no political power if you are seen as an underachiever. Second, you must be seen as vital to the success of the organization – and, yes, that is a different matter than doing your job well. You may be vital because of what you do, what you know, who you know, or even your past experiences *and* your ability to relate it to the organization's mission or current predicament. If, for example, your knowledge doesn't relate to the organization's mission or current predicament, you will not have much political power.

You can tell how much political power you have from how the informal network relates to you. Are you consulted more than others are? Have you become part of an inner circle? If your answer is 'yes', then you have political power. Now the question is to decide what to do with it! Use your political standing for good – for the good of your work, your department, and your organization. In order to keep your reputation intact and to be a person others want to work with, always look to do good.

Understand the words

Every organization has its own vocabulary, and in order to understand the organization, you must understand the words it uses. Technical organizations may produce a glossary of important terms, but it is likely that many ordinary sounding terms have unique meanings you must learn on the job. In addition, you will run into people who use words in a specific way, perhaps because of their responsibilities. For example, a manager once remarked during a staff meeting that the corporate library staff did an 'adequate' job. For most people, the word 'adequate' communicates 'less than outstanding', yet this manager's definition of 'adequate' was 'excellent'. Those who knew him had to interpret for others in the room to understand that he was giving a compliment.

Understanding the vocabulary of your organization will allow you to participate more appropriately in internal discussions by using the words others use with the 'accepted' meaning. How do you learn the vocabulary of your organization? Use your two ears and listen. Listen to how your colleagues use various expressions and assess the context in which they are used. When in doubt of a word's meaning, ask a trusted colleague for a definition.

Typically new words magically appear in an unclear context during meetings. If the discussion is not important to your work, make a note to ask for a definition after the meeting has concluded. If the word is critical to a discussion about your work, then politely interrupt and ask for clarity – an appropriate way gently to remind your colleagues that you are new to the organization and still learning its culture.

Create a common bond

Most organizations use language (common words and phrases) to create a common bond. In the 1980s many corporations adopted a set of quality principles that were used to elevate the standards used in the organization. The quality principles came with their own processes, rules, and vocabulary. Being able to use to vocabulary correctly meant that you had been through the training and were part of the 'club'.

Organizations want employees to feel as if they are part of the 'club' or part of the 'family'. Family members look out for each other and if you feel as if members of the organization are family, you will look out for them too, and do more to ensure the organization is successful. Perhaps you will work harder, be more protective of the organization's products and services, or even keep the organization's secrets. Such loyalty is important also because it means you will be more likely to hang in even when things get rough.

Deal with abuse

Although loyalty and a common bond create many positives for the organization, they do have a negative side. Some organizations will try to take advantage of or abuse loyal employees. You may be expected to work hard and perhaps even work long hours, and unreasonable demands can be a sign of an abusive organization. For example, an organization scheduling report due dates such that staff must work every holiday is being abusive. Dealing with abuse requires understanding your organization and understanding yourself.

First, does your organization actually tolerate abusive employees, abusive bosses, or abusive systems? If the answer is 'no', then you need to find the person who can act on your complaint. That person may be your boss, the boss of your boss, or someone in human resources. If you belong to a trade or professional union, you should contact your steward or someone with a similar role. Make sure you have documented the abuse and noted any witnesses who can corroborate your story. Reporting the abuse may be stressful, so you will need inner strength.

If your organization truly does tolerate abusive situations and considers them normal, then you need to assess how you want to respond. Several responses are possible depending on the situation including quitting, filing a lawsuit, or reporting the organization to an appropriate government agency. In some cases, you may want to seek legal advice before doing anything, especially if you believe you could take legal action against your employer. Whatever you do, do not be too rushed in your actions. Yes, you may want to quit, but you may quickly regret quitting on the spot rather than taking a more measured response.

One of our colleagues spent a long time in a work environment that was not conducive to her mental or physical health. In addition, she had a boss who could be supportive at times but was frequently verbally abusive. Although quitting would have provided immediate relief, it would have been difficult financially. She interviewed several attorneys and finally found one who felt right for her situation. The attorney helped her prepare for conversations with her boss, upper management, and human resources, and steered her away from potential 'potholes'. Negotiations for a graceful exit from the organization took several months and included discussions on what benefits the organization would provide after she left (and for how long) as well as what could be publicly said about her departure. During this time, our colleague relied on her own inner strength and the support of family and close friends to get her through the challenge. It was not easy, but she persevered and emerged successfully from the situation. We tell you this story not to scare you, but to help you understand that 'getting out' may take time.

Deal with conflict

A few people thrive on conflict, while the rest of us avoid conflict as if it were a disease. The truth is that every relationship and organization contains some conflict. It may take the form of competition, rivalry, or outright war. Each form, in an appropriate context, can energize an organization and cause it to be more creative. Competition or rivalries may spark new ideas, products, or services. An internal war – or battle – may shake up the organization in a positive way, although internal battles are usually destructive.

We are concerned here with the negative parts of conflict. It seems some people thrive on creating conflict, being agitators, and acting difficult. There are plenty of books and workshops on how to deal with difficult people, and we suggest you avail yourself of those resources. In fact, we recommend that you continue to learn throughout about dealing with conflict and difficult situations since the more techniques you learn, the better prepared you will be. Workshops are helpful in giving you a chance to practice newly acquired skills in a safe environment.

Our one piece of advice is that you do not take conflict as a personal assault, even when it seems to be. Once you see the conflict as being personal, your emotions will take over. Yes, it can be incredibly difficult to maintain emotional distance, and that is why we recommend seeking professional help.

A few dos, don'ts, and watch-outs

Here are pieces of advice our experience tells us are worthwhile in the context of navigating corporate cultures:

- Get to know as many people as possible in the organization, no matter what their job. Everyone has some influence to bring to bear on your behalf.

- During your breaks, take a walk through other areas of the building or complex. Doing so will give you an opportunity to interact with others in their environment and help to make you known to more people.

- Be conscious of the time you spend informally chatting with someone. It's best to keep your chats short unless you are indeed talking about work-related topics.

- When you interrupt someone, always ask if it is a good time to talk. If it is not, offer to arrange a conversation at a different time.

- Keep confidential information to yourself. You will want to be seen as someone who can be trusted so that people are comfortable sharing information with you.

- If you feel you must share something that has been told to you in confidence, share as little as possible and never disclose your source. Consider using confidential details to ask a question rather than making a statement. For example, 'what if we discontinued that service?' instead of 'I heard that we're going to discontinue that service!'

- Be willing to help others with their projects, if you have the time to do so. Volunteering your talents is a great way of getting known, building experience, and being seen as a can-do person.

- Recognize that the people you work with will become your friends, yet don't allow your friendships to interfere with your ability to do your job.

- Spending time with your colleagues – over coffee, lunch, or a drink after work – will allow you to get to know them better and build bonds that may help you as you advance in your career.

- Although it is easy to advise that you do not engage in romance at work, saying 'no' when your heart says 'yes' is impossible. Do not let your romance interfere with your work and do not be romantic at work.

- Do not date your boss or your employee. Doing either may cause colleagues to worry about favoritism. In some organizations, dating a subordinate may be strictly forbidden and may cost one of the parties his or her job.

- Recognize that the human resources department is there to help you, but be careful what you disclose. Although its staff members may seem (and be) helpful, it is their job to keep the best interests of the organization in mind. Do not assume information you give them to remain unshared with management.

- Stay up to date on what the organization's management is doing so as to ensure you understand how your services continue to relate to the organization's efforts.

- Do not assume you will automatically hear about everything your employer is doing or planning. If necessary, run searches periodically to find press releases and other public information about the organization.

The four rules of navigating corporate cultures

Years ago, a friend imparted some rules to Jill, rules learned by watching a highly effective business person. You may well see successful people around you implementing these rules, so why not try them yourself? They can help in any interaction with colleagues, customers, or suppliers.

You control your world

We tend to forget that we are in charge of our own destinies. We credit good situations to luck and blame bad situations on others. Yet we are each in control of our circumstances and surroundings. If you do not like what is occurring to you or around you, you have the power and responsibility to change it.

Find the person who will say 'yes'

Beneficial new ideas, products, and services are killed by the word 'no'. Those who say 'no' often provide valuable feedback and input, yet it is the word 'no' that sticks with us. Instead, learn from the rejections, make modifications to the idea, product, or service if necessary, then find the person who will say 'yes'. Such a person does exist, although he or she may not be your boss or even in your organization. Indeed, you may find it necessary to take your idea elsewhere in order to find someone who will approve it.

Be (gently) self-deprecating

Being self-deprecating can be indicative of low self-esteem because you are insinuating that you lack knowledge or abilities. However, with some people it may open doors. How? If you preface a suggestion by a reference to the listener's greater experience, you may reduce his or her resistance. For example, 'Of course you're the expert here, but I just wondered what would happen if we...' may get you heard where 'What about doing...' would not.

Be on the same level as, and fully engage with, the person in the conversation

It seems obvious and easy, but it isn't. If you are dealing with a CEO, student, engineer, or janitor interact on his or her level. Use appropriate language, examples, and so on. Note that using *appropriate* language does not imply using the *exact same* language as the other person. Be fully present in the conversation and make the other person your total focus for the duration of the interaction. The combination of focusing on others and interacting with them as their equal is very powerful – you demonstrate that you are interested in and want to understand their situation and motivations. In turn, they may take an interest in you and become your ally.

9

Winning support: 'selling' proposals with the business case approach

Many of our colleagues have indicated in various ways how surprised they were to learn through their careers how important it is to be skillful at the art of convincing. Getting others on board with a new way to do things, a new project, an investment, a particular hiring choice, changes in priorities – you name it – turned out to be much more challenging than they had believed. Rather than being no-brainers, the overhaul of the intranet, the launch of a needs assessment study, the usability test, or the feasibility investigation for digitizing an archival collection required a significant effort in persuasion before it was approved and funded. In other words, our colleagues and we have learned that advancing anything out of the established routine is a subtle and necessary skill.

One reason for the challenge is associated with the intangible nature of many of our activities. For example, it is impossible to prove in advance that a particular content management software will produce greater revenue than another or that policies for knowledge sharing will provide protection against risk. As we are typically working to facilitate and support the work and processes of others – as opposed to being involved directly in the 'business' of the organization – our advocacy for a given tool or project may be a stretch for others to understand, much less to support if significant investments are attached.

Crafting compelling proposals for superiors and being able to sell our ideas to peers is a significant career success factor not necessarily covered in graduate programs. We stress it here because we are certain most readers will sooner or later need to produce a document or presentation to advance an idea, or need to influence opinion in subtler ways such as building grassroots support. In addition, we know that in volunteer or association work it is essential to be persuasive to overcome the natural limitations typical of such work and to make leadership positions effective.

But don't good ideas sell themselves?

The short answer is a resounding no. Good ideas may happen to arrive at a decision maker's doorstep just at the right time with just the right set of appealing characteristics, but the foundation for creating convincing arguments is the realization that decision makers do not agree to proposals because we think they are cool. Decision makers weigh their options, assess how closely a new idea or proposed investment or project aligns with existing or new priorities, and make their choices based on what in their view is most likely to produce a desirable outcome at the lowest risk or cost. Said another way: some executives may go with gut feel or passion for a cause, but most decision makers look at *what makes business sense.* As a result, we are required to advocate for our ideas and projects not with appeals to emotions but rather with objective descriptions of realistic expectations: if X is invested, Y is the likely result.

Convincing team or committee members to support a new idea similarly requires work to demonstrate the benefits for them of supporting us. It is generally accepted that getting one's mind around a new concept – and certainly if it involves a change in normal routine, a learning curve, and similar adjustment – requires mental energy; when we advance a suggestion to colleagues, we need to provide the enticement for them to put out that energy.

Subtle dynamics are sometimes at play when it comes to making others 'come around to our way of thinking'. Human nature at times seems to prefer the status quo – because it is familiar, not because it is the better option – and people therefore often need a little push to get behind an idea or new venture beyond saying 'it sounds good in theory'. In some teams, there may be a communal 'don't upset the applecart' mentality leading to an instinctive hesitation when someone proposes something new. In others – according to our experience – there could be a sense of questioning: 'who is she and why does she think she can just come here and suggest change?' The latter could be the case especially if the proponent is new to a team.

As a contrary phenomenon, we sometimes see people who are eager to be associated with the latest cool technology or hot fad. It is just as untoward when team members rush into 'sexy' side projects without assessment of the investments, ramifications, and potential outcomes as it is when they resist needed change.

Therefore, we are advocates of a logical and impersonal approach relying strictly on the merits of what is being proposed – in other words, the business case approach.

What is the business case approach?

The business case approach rests on a dispassionate assessment of the desirability, in the minds of decision makers or team mates *and* in light of the overall organizational priorities, of a particular solution to a challenge, proposal for improvement, or other suggestion for change of status quo. The assessment takes into consideration the motivations of managers and executives given their goals and the organization's current status, and it recognizes that what to the proponents of a new idea is an exciting opportunity may to senior managers be but one more in a collection of competing requests for funding. Further, it recognizes that a group of peers may be reluctant to support change because 'it sounds like work'.

The business case approach starts with an overview of the motivations of decision makers and moves through a logical progression of questions whose answers provide a foundation for choosing a course of action. It is essential that readers (or listeners if the case is made in person) are able to recognize the initial description of the current situation, agree that remedial action (or taking advantage of an opportunity) is desirable, are reassured that other organizations are or have been in the same boat, and so on – in other words, the business case progression, like any sales process, seeks the buyer's nod at every step of the way up until the 'yes, let's go'. The steps in the business case progression are shown in Table 1.

Steps in the business case progression

	The question is…	The business case approach addresses…	It is expected/hoped the readers or listeners think…
1	What is the problem, need, or opportunity (PNO) we are concerned about?	Reasons why the status quo is unsatisfactory or risky, and potential consequences of failing to take action; or – if there is no pressing problem – reasons why the circumstances are favorable to take advantage of an opportunity	Yes, it's true we have that problem Yes, we do need to… Yes, we ought to strike while the opportunity is there
2	What interests, concerns, aspirations, and motivations of those who will make the decision – in light of the current circumstances and environment – should be recognized?	Relevant considerations such as external pressures (e.g. legislative or market developments), internal conditions (e.g. staff retirements, new technology), and competitive or comparative considerations (e.g. what is happening in competing or analogous organizations)	It's good that the pressures we are under have been understood It's reassuring that the market conditions and other external realities are factored in from the beginning
3	What can be learned from an environmental scan – what are other organizations doing about similar PNOs?	Lessons learned from initiatives in similar settings and pointers to success factors and risks	Impressive how the homework was done to find out how other organizations in the field are dealing with…
4	What options are realistic and what are the respective pros and cons?	The range of reasonable options applicable given the above and given the current budgetary situation, and the features of each	OK, now we are interested in seeing what options are on the table… and what the pros and cons are for each

Steps in the business case progression (*Cont'd*)

5	What option is proposed?	The preferred option, in more detail and with operational implications	Let's look at that option in more detail
6	What is the investment?	The financial and operational costs and other relevant ramifications (e.g. a reorganization of staff) and anticipated risk mitigation	Such costs are reasonable, and it's good to see that risks have been addressed up front
7	What is the return on investment (ROI) and the key benefits?	Direct ROI – if it can be established in cost savings or additional earnings – and indirect benefits such as increased efficiency, competitiveness, or similar attainments deemed meaningful	These benefits are definitely worth working for, even if it means some temporary disruption, learning curves, and so on
8	How is the proposed option aligned with organizational directions?	The 'fit' or relationship between the organization's existing strategic goals and the proposed option	In addition, the proposal is in line with the established priorities (so if we approve, we will look good)
9	Is the organization ready to proceed?	Whether or not the organization is in a position to proceed or whether measures need to be taken in advance	It's reassuring that we are in a position to proceed with little or no delay or preparatory cost
10	Is there background information or data to support the case we are making?	Existing operational evidence, professional literature, statistics, benchmark information, and other factual material to lend credibility	It's even more reassuring that the background data backs up the proposal

What does a business case document look like?

The organizational culture – and the relationship between the proponent and the decision maker – dictates whether a one-page memo suffices or whether a detailed document complete with operational evidence and benchmark measures from other enterprises is required.

In a situation where the proponent is relatively unknown or unproven in the eyes of the decision maker, considerable documentation and backup data may be needed. When the proponent is a well-established and trusted source of advice, briefer instruments may do the job.

Given the reality that most decision makers have limited time, a well-proven format involves an ultra brief exposé of one to three pages followed by a narrative description of seven to eight pages backed up by 'the full version' document of any length, complete with appendices.

Here is a greatly simplified example of a brief business case memorandum addressing the need to redesign an intranet from the ground up. For the purposes of illustration and the focus on the progression of the argument, we leave out detail and additional options that would likely be present in a 'real life' memorandum:

Date
To: VP, Corporate Services, ABC Inc (or ABC Association or ABC Government Department)
From: Manager, Intranet
Re: Proposal to invest in a redesign and rebuild of the intranet

For discussion at the upcoming departmental status meeting

---

1 Background

Our corporate intranet was launched in the early days of web technology and has undergone considerable evolution in its lifetime. At the outset, it was state of the art and widely admired; by now, it is rich in content and challenging to use as a result of numerous additions and enhancements in functionality over time. The intranet team receives a growing number of negative comments and complaints (rising by about 10% each month). A typical complaint states: 'It is virtually impossible to find information we know is in fact held on the intranet. Much time is spent in vain navigating the increasingly confusing interface and consulting with colleagues we suspect might happen to have a copy of the document we are looking for.'

I am concerned that without proactive work to deliver a contemporary intranet with intuitive navigability and search functionality on a par with the software capability our knowledge workers see every day on the public internet, they may give up on our intranet entirely, thus engaging in risky and time consuming activities to find the information they need (such as storing documents 'just in case' on flash drives so that no one can know what is the official version of a document or – worse – so that no one actually finds a key document because it is 'lost').

2 Context

In light of the increasing productivity pressures occasioned by retirement and staff turnover, and given the industry's growing competitiveness, it is essential that we support our knowledge workers in being as effective as possible in supporting ABC's strategic goals and short and long-term deliverables. ABC can ill afford for highly educated – and expensive to recruit – specialty staff to waste time because of something as mundane as an outdated and user-unfriendly intranet.

3 Environmental scan and benchmarks

Today's standards for intranets are well documented in the technical literature and at conferences (see Appendix 1). In addition, my team has conducted benchmark interviews with webmasters at [names of relevant organizations] and verified that they have all rebuilt their intranets within the last 18 months, obtaining not only positive feedback but also measurable productivity improvements (see Appendix 2). Key considerations involve a design allowing for smooth integration of new technology and software for the foreseeable future.

4 Options considered

My team and I have developed a matrix showing the pros and cons of three possible options:

Option	Advantages	Risks
1. Freeze current intranet while team develops new one	▪ No extra cost ▪ Staff are familiar with needs and current complaints	▪ Already disaffected users could abandon faith altogether and be unwilling to try using the new intranet
2. Keep current intranet operating at maintenance level; engage consulting team to design/build/install new one and support transfer of content	▪ Collaboration between our staff and expert external team will yield optimal design ▪ Our staff leverage knowledge about ABC to focus on preserving key content ▪ Speedy implementation	▪ No significant risks
3. Compromise: engage design team to create blueprint for team to implement	▪ Lower out of pocket cost than option 2	▪ Implementation could prove challenging for my staff because they must also deal with day to day tasks ▪ Delays could hinder uptake of new intranet

5 The recommended option

Option 2 yields the greatest value for the out of pocket costs and addresses the serious productivity losses currently experienced by delivering a new intranet in the shortest possible time. The savings to be realized from option 3 are unlikely to warrant the risk of a protracted implementation phase.

6 Investment

According to industry standards and informal estimates obtained through contacts, the investment envelope for option 2 is in the range of X to Y – about Z% of what ABC is currently investing in mobile devices. The involvement of my staff, though of course essential, is modest and focuses on guiding the designers about ABC's needs. My staff will need to be involved extensively in the installment and content transfer phases and as a benefit will gain immediate familiarity with the operation of the new intranet.

7 Benefits

By taking decisive action and dealing concretely with a highly visible irritant, ABC will not only support its knowledge workers' productivity but also set in place the foundation for future upgrades that will be seamless and cause no service interruption.

8 Organizational alignment

Knowledge worker productivity is a key challenge described in the latest annual report and a key goal featured in the strategic plan. Installing a state of the art, non-proprietary platform to allow my staff to keep up with evolving technology in supporting effectiveness and efficiency over the long term will pay off immediately and sustainably.

9 Ability to proceed

My team has extensive knowledge of reputable consulting firms (see Appendix 3) with track records in building and installing intranets similar to ABC's and – in voluntary overtime – has developed a draft RFP and business requirements document. With your approval, we are ready to issue the finalized RFP within a week and expect that the evaluation process would entail a project start approximately eight weeks later. Based on the extensive experience of the firms in question, I predict a launch of the new intranet approximately four months after start.

10 Appendices

Appendix 1: List of Relevant Articles and Conference Presentations
Appendix 2: Benchmark Findings: The Intranets at DEF, GHI, and JKL
Appendix 3: Descriptions of Proposed Firms to Receive the RFP

Business cases for info pros: here's why, here's how
Information Today, 2008, ISBN: 978-57387-335-2

After decades of working with colleagues dealing with the challenge of winning support for their proposals, Ulla produced a concise guide to the art of developing business case documents. Reviews are available at *www.destricker.com* under 'Books'.

If money isn't involved – what about grassroots support for an idea or initiative?

Even if you aren't seeking approval of a financial investment, you still need influence skills and persuasive arguments to foster the kind of thinking and mental buy-in you are after. For example, you may wish to introduce a more collegial attitude in a team, foster a stronger emphasis on customer service, advocate the appropriate use of social media to gain visibility among a stakeholder community, enhance the professional look of the materials your team produces, and so on. Although such goals may not require RFPs and direct outlays, they sure call for effort – and more than anything else, they require a hefty dose of credibility and social capital on the part of the advocate.

The management literature is replete with material on how to gain influence without authority. A key theme, one we believe is particularly relevant for information professionals working in environments characterized by collegial rather than hierarchical management styles, is the use of reputation and respect as a lever in giving others reason to pay attention and give thought to what we say. Hence, the first order of business for any information professional is to work on building a ballast of professional credibility. Such a ballast consists of not only a reputation for technical expertise but also the esteem colleagues have for us; we want for them to regard us as thoughtful, dependable, and dedicated professionals devoted to serving stakeholders. With that ballast, we have a better chance to influence others at the grassroots level.

How are credibility and social capital built?

In Chapter 4 we discuss professional brand and common challenges associated with organizational dynamics. Here, we focus on building credibility and social capital in the workplace you are currently in. Key elements include:

- accomplishments in priority projects or projects garnering attention in other ways
- deliverables visible to key people and teams
- supporting colleagues in unusual or emergency situations
- proactive work to support the team
- going the extra mile for a colleague
- stepping up to the plate when crises warrant
- showing compassion and kindness toward others.

Common to those elements are integrity, reliability, and discretion – gossipers don't tend to gain or keep anyone's respect.

I'm so glad we talked!

Many are the occasions Ulla remembers where a casual conversation moved to cover a topic of importance in a relaxed atmosphere:

I was unaware, but now that I know, I will...

My team is drafting a white paper on it – could you send a memo?

Oh, if that is the case, I'll alert my team.

I could put you in touch with...

Do you know Sophia? – She's involved in a similar initiative and I think you should meet.

I happen to have a report you might find helpful.

Please stay in touch, we may need to coordinate once the project advances.

Such conversations are common among colleagues who each have social capital and credibility to put behind their comments.

What does grassroots persuasion 'look like'?

Advocacy and persuasion is often subtle and incremental – accumulated over time through casual conversations in the hallway, in a cafeteria line, or over coffee or lunch. Influence may be stronger when it is introduced quietly, one person at a time, and as a by-the-way based on mutual trust, rather than as a campaign or crusade.

We hasten to stress that grassroots influence has nothing to do with behind-the-scenes scheming, political manouvering, or plotting to thwart an upcoming change. It refers simply to the activity of making others more aware of options and their consequences to put them in a better position to decide for themselves what priorities they support.

Therefore, grassroots persuasion tends to begin with asking 'what do you think?', followed by careful listening. It is much easier to get others on board when we understand their thinking and concerns and thus are able to address specific points when we once again touch on the subject at hand.

Naturally, everything we say in order to encourage others to adopt a particular opinion is based on and backed up by evidence – just as in the formal business case. When the messages we communicate resonate with the recipients as supporting the overall benefit of the team, the department, and the organization as a whole, we enhance the likelihood that others will pay attention to what we are saying.

Received wisdom on grassroots influence

It is generally understood that it is ill advised to spring surprises or introduce new material in a meeting without giving everyone time to prepare. Regardless of whether you are in attendance, it is helpful to ensure attendees are oriented in advance about what may come up and about the relevant facts, considerations, concerns, and potential objections. Equipping everyone ahead of time with pertinent information goes a long way toward achieving a suitable decision at a meeting.

Similarly, it is wise to plan far ahead when working to influence others. It is easy to underestimate the length of time it takes for a viewpoint or preference to gain acceptance or for people to change their minds about something or someone. In movies, it's common to see a scene in which one remark sets off dramatic change; in reality – although one dynamite presentation may indeed sway everyone immediately – it may take many conversations and months on end before general attitudes shift.

Decisions happen outside meetings

Early in Jill's career she believed that decisions were taken in meetings. Isn't that why we have them? In fact, all the work you do to create a business case for a decision will be presented during a meeting, but it should also have been discussed informally before the meeting occurs to ensure the information is not a surprise to anyone. In addition, it helps you understand what people need to know in order to make their decisions. You may find that you have not yet made a compelling case and need to do more work. Most importantly, it helps you build support before the meeting occurs.

Unless the information is confidential, use coffee breaks and informal conversations to give decision makers a quick overview of the upcoming decision. Although you will want to convince them immediately of your point of view, it is better if you listen to their concerns and questions, then use the input to help build a better case. If you are asked questions you cannot answer, take time to find the answers and be ready to discuss them in your next informal conversation.

How far in advance do you need to start talking about a future decision? It may depend on the importance of the decision and the amount of support needed for it. You may want to start informal conversations days or weeks in advance. Since they are informal, they may require just the right opportunity to occur, and that could take time.

Over the years, Jill has used many informal chats over coffee – or just standing in the hallway – to test a new idea, build support for a decision, or ensure everyone agrees with what needs to be done. These conversations have in addition helped others know what she is doing and see value in her work.

The 'business case in reverse': demonstrating existing value

As a result of the intangible nature of much of the work information professionals do, they often find themselves needing to demonstrate that it is worthwhile maintaining the organizational investment in their work. In a manner of speaking, they must make the business case for themselves over and over, in the face of pressures to cut costs, by corralling evidence of the positive results arising from their salaries, tools, content, and so on.

Unfortunately, that is a significant challenge at the best of times, and many an information professional can recount the tale of being viewed as superfluous 'now that everything is on the internet'. The fact that information-related conference programs are full of sessions dealing with strategies for demonstrating value indicates we will likely always need to make the business case.

In some settings, value can be demonstrated at least in part through measurable indicators such as 'decrease in time required to perform a vision test' or 'increase in average grades obtained by high school students'. Traditionally, information professionals have made a habit of tracking activities; a simple example from the past is the number of public library book loans or museum visits being used to support requests for municipal funding. Although information professionals may have plenty of measurable indicators – say, number of interactions with knowledge workers or number of visits to a corporate wiki – such statistics frequently have little meaning for executives looking to reduce budgets. Even worse, statistics such as 'number of publications added to the collection' or 'number of scanned pages added to the repository' not only tend to be unenlightening for decision makers (is that number good, bad, or indifferent... should it have been higher or lower?) but in fact ask people to question why we need that collection or repository in the first place.

Statistics, therefore, must be collected and presented with care. Is a growing number of page views in a particular section of the intranet a sign of its utility or of the fact that users are confused? Does a sudden decrease in page views indicate that content is no longer valuable or simply that a given project is now complete? We suggest that information professionals adopt as a mantra: 'Never offer an activity measure without the accompanying story!'

The testimonial evidence

So how do information professionals demonstrate their value? The hard way, through qualitative assessment of the impact they had or are having on the business processes of the organizations they serve. Substantiating the business case for maintaining our services amounts to a description of a hypothetical situation: 'According to the testimony of the analysts, engineers, chemists, or economists (etc.), the following undesirable outcomes would likely arise if we information professionals weren't here.'

We cannot stress sufficiently the necessity and significance of the qualitative assessment. Statements like 'Without the information we got from the information center, we would have incurred a significant risk by...' or 'We easily cut time to market by six months due to the competitive intelligence work of the information center' must be front and center in the annual reports and reverse business cases we produce.

Day in and day out, every month and every year, we information professionals must devote time to gauge the impact we have. Satisfaction polls attached to deliveries of research results may yield impressive measures if 90% of respondents check off the radio button for *extremely helpful*... but we need more. In essence, we need to be in perpetual audit mode: 'what difference did our contribution make for your team in terms of time savings, confidence in decision making, quality of deliverables and so on?', and we need to document them meticulously.

The bottom line is that evidence of the value of information professionals' work must come from those engaged in the business of the organization. The scientists or the sales teams must speak up for it, and unless we ask them to, they may never think to offer up their appreciative opinion. A constantly updated file of testimonials from opinion leaders, revenue generators, and other key individuals is a must for every information services manager.

But what if the organizational culture demands numbers rather than testimonials? Let's use the business case approach again, this time to show return on investment in information support.

The ROI calculation

In the interest of clarity, the example below is simplistic, focusing only on the cost of staff time; the intent is to show how it is possible to extrapolate impact estimates from the intrinsically non-measurable impact of information professionals' work.

The setting is a scientific or technical research organization and the scenario is a potential significant cut – by 50% – in the information staff supporting the researchers. It must be shown what (undesirable) impact such a cut would have.

As preparation, the information services team leader has conducted a series of interviews with researchers to clarify their typical behavior when they look for information to feed their research projects. Making sure to explain that the interviews are 'not about how much you respect us but rather what impact our work has on yours', the team leader assembled the following data.

Base

On average 100 researchers need new literature, statistics, or results of academic projects, and so on four times per month or 4,400 times in every 11-month working year.

First, we look at time investment and time savings realized through the information professionals. Then, we look at the additional time spent making up for information not found.

Time savings

The 50 researchers in Group A are in the habit of doing their own searching and report that each search averages four hours. They spend a collective [50 × 4 searches × 4 hrs × 11 months =] *8,800 hours* per year in pursuit of information. At an estimated hourly cost of $50, that works out to *$440,000*.

The 50 researchers in Group B use the services of the information center and report that each search averages 30 minutes because they start with the search results found by the information professionals and simply do some verifying and fine tuning. They spend a collective [50 × 4 searches × 0.5 hours × 11 months =] *1,100 hours* per year in pursuit of information. At an estimated hourly cost of $50, that works out to *$55,000*. The information professionals serving Group B report that each search takes 1.5 hours for a total of [50 × 4 searches × 1.5 hours × 11 months =] *3,300 hours*. At an estimated hourly cost of $35, that works out to *$115,500*.

Hence the math looks like this:

- Group A cost of search = $440,000

- Group B cost of search = $55,000 + $115,500 = $170,500

- Difference: use of information professionals saves the organization $269,500 per year – and frees up 7,700 hours for Group B researchers to devote to work other than searching – a time value of $385,000 but likely a much greater value of the achievements Group B can deliver.

Making up for information not found

Group A members report that in 25% of searches they miss important information and end up compensating by putting in 30 extra hours of work – doing additional searching, redoing experiments, talking to colleagues to resolve gaps, and so on. Hence:

- 25% of [50 × 4 searches × 11 months] = 550 searches each cause 30 extra hours of work = 16,500 'lost' hours per year that could have been devoted to other work. At $50/hr, that's a cost of $825,000 going toward making up for not using the services of information professionals.

- If Group A members were to take up the habits of Group B and use the information center – a new cost of $115,500 – the annual gain for the organization in avoiding lost hours would be $709,500.

Needless to say, a calculation like this one will be subject to challenge – what about serendipity, how do we know the information professionals didn't miss important information, and so on. In our experience, however, setting out time consumption in this manner may help focus executives' minds on the cost of how subject matter specialists spend their time.

Received wisdom on impact and ROI measures

Gathering indicators of impact is time consuming and often frustrating – especially if one is overwhelmed by the 'real' work. That said, we cannot afford to ignore the requirement to be ready at all times to produce evidence that our salaries pay themselves back to our organization many times over.

A strategy of saying 'sorry, we are insufficiently staffed to help you' has the apparent potential to draw attention to an imbalance between demand and capacity, but may backfire as clients who were not helped may never return and may never ask management how come they could not be served. It may work appropriately if there is a solid relationship between the information services manager and influential representatives from the business areas of the organization (those who typically get what they want) so that pressure to sustain or increase the funding for the information services unit comes from a source that is difficult for executives to ignore.

10

Making the leap to a managerial role: being the boss

We have heard – and lived – several variations on the comment 'Of all the things I did in my career... managing people was the most difficult' – and we agree that being the boss – that is, having the responsibility to make decisions impacting the work lives of our staff members – entails a great many situations whose resolutions are anything but straightforward.

In Chapter 15, we describe some major learning points in our careers, touching on the theme that skills required of those who are in charge of teams are not always covered in graduate programs and must be acquired on the job. In that context, we recognize that even though someone might have sat us down at an early stage and said 'now listen, here's what you need to know about being a manager' we may not have been in a position to understand the depth of what was explained.

Now that we are seasoned and able to speak from our own experience, we are able to call your attention to aspects of managerial work you may want to keep in mind as you observe your own bosses 'doing management'. We can't tell you what to do... but we can encourage you to be sensitive and observant in order to prepare for the day when it's your turn to move on from being one of the gang to being in charge.

A management role is not a must

It is common for professionals to aspire to get promoted or land jobs at a higher level fairly regularly throughout their careers. However, there is nothing wrong with being content to do professional work without the responsibilities of being the boss. If that applies to you, consider discussing your preference with your supervisor so that he or she may factor it into planning. For example, some of our colleagues express a fondness for managing *projects* as opposed to managing *people*. That said, consider as well that over time you may grow more comfortable with the idea of managing.

What is the definition of 'manager'?

Being a manager and being a leader are not synonymous. Anyone can be a leader regardless of his or her job title – to prove it, our profession is full of leaders who inspire their colleagues, pioneer association programs, and contribute to the collective knowledge of practitioners. It is to be hoped that managers have leadership skills, and we encourage all our readers to read up on the literature on leadership. Management, on the other hand, is a discipline focusing on planning and ensuring resources for the operations of a department or organization, delivering results, meeting performance quotas, handling unforeseen events, shaping position descriptions and hiring staff, and making sure staff members have the skills and tools they need for their jobs.

Typically, managers have strategic or performance goals toward which they are expected to work. For example, they may be expected to achieve certain transformations or financial goals over a time horizon while they keep services going. It is essential before assuming a managerial role to be aware whether its goals are imposed from above or whether the incumbent has latitude to set the goals.

The skills exercised by a good manager may include only a portion of the technical and professional expertise with which he or she entered a first job. Yes, it is helpful when the manager has 'been there' and remembers what it was like to be on the front lines answering client questions, manage an intranet or content management system, administer digital rights, and so on, but it is not a prerequisite for succeeding in managing a department or organization. A good manager will always make sure to have a sufficient level of insight into the operational details and day to day challenges and will involve the staff members responsible for operations in the discussions forming the basis for planning.

A special kind of managerial role is the 'acting manager' or 'interim manager' whose responsibilities are to keep operations running smoothly while a search is on for a permanent manager. Such a role may be a stepping stone for someone who is not sure about wanting to move into management ranks.

What does a manager 'do'?

It could be said that managers don't *do* – they *enable others to do*. Although they might in a pinch, managers don't construct code for web-based services or handle the fragile volumes being scanned for the digitization project; they don't perform literature searches or teach incoming undergrads about the academic resources available; and so on. Instead, they deal with budgets, personnel matters, interdepartmental or interorganizational coordination, long range planning, and other similar tasks that may strike younger information professionals as being removed from the 'core' of the professional skills they worked so hard to acquire during their MLIS studies.

A typical manager deals with people, produces reports, and attends meetings. As a result of the amount of time spent in meetings, actual work – for example, producing reports or plans – takes place, you guessed it, evenings and weekends. Managers are not paid by the hour – they are paid to deliver results.

A common to-do list for a manager could be something like this:

- Request recent operational statistics for upcoming budget kickoff meeting – discuss any adjustments or new measures with staff

- Meet with Peter S. to discuss his performance review next month

- Prepare presentation for consortium meeting on plans for ILS upgrade vs. switch to open source ILS

- Meet with intranet team to discuss potential reorganization of resource pages

- Prepare two scenarios in draft plan for next fiscal year for next week's management meeting

- Sort out vacation schedules – check with HR re overtime compensation policy

- Organize retirement event for Charlotte P.

- Meet with physical facilities coordinator regarding reconfiguration of south offices

- Investigate offsite storage options for records 7+ years

- Find consultants to conduct needs assessment and assist with long range strategic plan – what are the standard parameters?

- Call Lisa R. in to discuss concerns raised by colleagues
- Finalize license with vendors A, B, and C
- Work with staff committee to review proposal for changing format and timing of staff meetings

It is immediately obvious that a manager's scope of work ranges widely and requires if not expertise in, then some awareness of, such esoteric matters as building and fire codes, HR basics, records management, statistics and budgets, and licensing of electronic content. What may be less obvious is the fact that a considerable amount of interpersonal finesse, tact, and communication with individuals and groups is needed as well.

The vast number of books dealing with management might suggest there are 'recipes' or 'recommended approaches' for working as a manager. Don't be fooled – being a successful manager does not mean taking direction from books (as Ulla mistakenly, briefly, believed early in her career). Rather, it requires sensitivity, openness, a willingness to admit mistakes, and a knack for gaining the trust of staff members.

Typical management challenges

Common to many managerial positions are challenges clustered around time, dealing with staff, and developing staff. For example:

- juggling time to attend meetings, paying attention to what's going on 'on the floor', and being available to deal with unforeseen matters
- being supportive of staff members needing extra support (without being seen as favoring some individuals over others)

- making and implementing decisions that may be unpopular among the team members for any number of reasons (including a reluctance to change)

- simultaneously managing 'down' by supporting the teams and 'up' by communicating effectively with and advancing proposals to executives

- spotting talent and coordinating tasks or projects to groom team members interested in growing their skills.

How can one learn to become a (better) manager? There has to be a way!

Good question! We believe there are many avenues for picking up managerial skills. One available to everyone from the first day in an entry level job is to observe. Observe how the team leaders and department managers behave and communicate, and assess what behaviors and communication styles appear effective – or not! – vis à vis the teams and departments being managed. Observe the dynamics of the interaction between peers in a group by themselves, between a group of peers in the presence of the manager, and between individual staff members and a manager. Consider some of the possible reasons for exchanges appearing 'odd' in some way; for example, could insecurity on the part of a new manager lead to some defensiveness and could long experience on the part of a staff member lead to some impatience with a new manager who 'doesn't understand how it works'?

Here are some suggestions for how to increase your managerial insight:

- By all means read widely – every article and book has ideas to offer.

- Look for and attend management oriented workshops and sessions at professional events.

- Discuss challenges with colleagues in the network (as in 'have you ever...?' or 'what would you do if...?').

- Find a mentor with whom you can discuss challenges you encounter as a manager.

Volunteering to head up projects and special event teams is a good way to dip one's toes into managerial waters.

What you need: basic skills

In any professional role, technical skills in certain areas are taken for granted. In a managerial role, they are essential. We list them here to remind you to work on acquiring them from the first day on your first job.

Understand finance

We must understand budgets and balance sheets and basic financial concepts such as accrual, deferred revenue, overhead allocation, and calculation of internal service chargebacks. It is essential to be familiar with the organization's policies on managing the budget (for example, is it alright to transfer funds from one line item to another across cost types – in other words, can you use money set aside to pay for licenses to send a staff member to a conference?). Similarly, it is essential to know how to provide for contingencies without raising red flags that we are 'tucking excess money away'.

Understand statistics

Communicating to one's immediate supervisor and preparing material for presentation further up the line requires knowing what to count, how to count it, and how to present the numbers. In the positions typically held by information professionals, it is a particular challenge to determine meaningful activity measures and operational gauges and to extrapolate the impact and value of the work performed. Tracking the number of hits to certain pages on the intranet may be a perfectly legitimate method for assessing their value to users, but it could be argued, for example, that some hits occur simply because users are confused and click on a tab because they misunderstand its purpose. Monitoring the number of inquiries received via email may be helpful as an indicator of a shift in demand for telephone coverage; be sure always to explain why something is counted and what it means when a number increases, decreases, or remains unchanged.

Be able to manage projects

From the most innocent sounding task ('let's move the shared printer over there') to obviously complex undertakings ('the entire archives must be moved to a new facility next year'), all projects require planning, organization, coordination, and impact assessment and mitigation. We have all heard the stories of perfectly executed projects with impactful flaws: no one measured the length of the cable, so in the ideal new spot the printer had no power (until a longer one was procured); or a misunderstanding in the design of the new building necessitated last-minute work to devise a new solution for a workspace.

Know how to write proposals and reports

Skills in persuasion are so critical that we provided the previous chapter to deal with them. It is essential for a manager to be able to produce documents that are clear, easy to read, and effective in communicating a message. Skills are needed in crafting and developing an argument, and in using the features of the word processing program to take advantage of such text enhancers as tables and charts.

Craft and give presentations

All managers will sooner or later be called on to present plans to staff, proposals to committees, business cases to executives, sales material to potential buyers, and so on. It is essential to master the art of presenting information in person using the props most suitable for the matter at hand (not always a slide show!) – in an engaging, convincing manner. If standing up to speak has you weak in the knees, we recommend Toastmasters as an excellent source of techniques for delivering powerful presentations.

Be able to manage human resources

Managing people is a subtle and demanding art, often tripping up individuals who otherwise thought of themselves as 'people people'. Here are some illustrations of the ways in which managers must demonstrate knowledge and finesse:

- Know the law. Everything a manager does must fit within employment legislation.
- Know how to delegate without dumping. Determining what tasks can be delegated and then handing them over smoothly to a team member may be trickier than it sounded at first.

- Avoid micromanaging *and* abandoning. It is well known how much staff members dislike being checked on and interfered with constantly, and managers are well advised to give their teams direction and then let them get on with the job. However, an overly hands-off approach could leave a team feeling left out in the cold. It's always advised to consult directly with a team's members to determine how much additional support and engagement they (no longer) need.

- Don't fall back into comfort zones. Once promoted or hired into a management role, assume it. Sure, you may pitch in should there be a backlog to get through, but every hour spent doing a technical task is an hour not spent managing.

What you need: personal abilities

Some people have reputations as 'natural born managers' and we suspect this may be due to their personalities. The following behavioral characteristics seem to make for success in a management role, based on our observations.

Be approachable, compassionate, and inspiring

We often hear colleagues say how much they enjoy working – and going the extra mile – for a manager who is friendly, considerate, understanding, and visionary. It may well be easier for team members to accept tough-but-necessary policy changes when they are communicated skillfully by a manager who clearly demonstrates understanding of the tradeoffs involved and their impacts on each person on the team.

Project positive authority

Being a friendly manager does not mean being buddies with those we manage. (In fact, being too close with selected members of the team can be counterproductive as it may be seen as favoritism.) As the manager, your job is to manage – not to be popular. Keep your compassion, but also your composure – your team members need to see you firmly in charge and on top of whatever may befall the department.

Earn the trust of the troops

As we ourselves experienced, earned trust is a powerful instrument for getting things done by our teams. When team members trust a manager to be fair, to consider all sides of a matter before deciding, to go to bat with executives when necessary, and so on, they tend to perform much better than they would without the security of knowing 'the boss always comes through with what is best for the organization overall'.

A unique challenge: being promoted from a team to manage it

The special situation in which a team member is plucked to become the manager of former colleagues is so difficult that alternatives are often pursued, for example by transferring the star performer to lead a different team. The difficulty is rooted in the awkwardness inherent in having a person move from being a peer to being a superior – an awkwardness felt equally by the promoted individual and the former equals. Should it happen to you, keep these tips in mind:

- Prepare for some time of adjustment as your former peers sort out how to act around you and find out how best to communicate with you.

- Do not apologize verbally or through any other behavior. You were selected for the job – now you must carry it out. Assume your new role with dignity yet without artificial distance that could be interpreted as arrogance.

- Do not suddenly become a different person from the one you were. Your former colleagues will see right through it and won't know when you believe in what you are saying and when you are projecting opinions you think you ought to have.

- Accept that you will lose the camaraderie you once had with the team.

Reap the rewards

Just as we know how challenging it is to be the manager, we know how rewarding it can be. It is deeply satisfying to lead a team through a project and watch it deliver an ambitious goal, and it is a thrill to see a staff member learn through coaching to stretch his or her competencies. We promise that from every managerial role you will take away extremely worthwhile lessons and grow as a person.

How would you manage?

In typical scenarios like the ones below, what would you do?

1 You have launched a strategic outreach program to educate knowledge workers in the organization about the full range of services available from the information specialists. The two eager team members you selected to set up and conduct the orientation sessions are doing well, but their regular workload, originally taken on by the colleagues with their full agreement, is piling up faster than anticipated. Short of halting the outreach program, what options would you consider?

2 According to budget restrictions, only one team member can receive reimbursement for the costs of attending the major annual professional conference. A has previously attended and always brings back valuable new insights to share with the team; B is a recent addition and is being mentored by A. Ideally, they ought to attend the conference together. How would you solve the dilemma?

3 Supporting the clientele's needs for competitive intelligence requires constant vigilance and surveillance using the internet to monitor for relevant blog posts, forums, social media, white papers, conference presentations, and so on. However, two team members – both excellent workers – have been observed spending 'more than a few' minutes tending to their personal affairs outside lunch hour, and the rest of the team are getting resentful – not only of the slackers, but of you as well for not dealing with it head on. What to do?

4 A retirement has created an opportunity for a promotion from within. A is 'in line' for the position while B is more suited for it. If you bypass A, how could you ensure he or she stays motivated? If you promote A, what consequences do you risk?

11

Resilience at work: coping when things get tough

In every work environment, challenges and difficulties will present themselves from time to time. Workloads may spike extremely to produce fatigue, technology transitions may cause disruption and stress, interpersonal conflict may cause a tense atmosphere, and so on. It is realistic to expect periods during which our enthusiasm for getting to work is dampened.

That said, we offer some suggestions for adopting a constructive and positive attitude for 'tough times' and for determining whether to abandon a situation proving intractable. We do so on the basis of our experience and of many discussions with colleagues over the years. Our fundamental approach is to apply understanding of one's own preferences and inclinations, to attempt to see things from the point of view of others, and to give every reasonable effort to produce a desirable outcome – but to honor ourselves sufficiently to depart if our efforts cannot succeed.

It's tough all over – let's pull together

With every new year, there are new economic and political circumstances, new technology options, and evolving demographics to create an ever changing set of workplace scenarios impinging on how we feel getting out of bed to go to work and how we experience the work day. It's worth considering the influence of overall conditions on the 'feel' of a workplace: a reduced budget is unlikely to be a result of anyone's whim; a canceled project may have been perfectly desirable last year but may be unaffordable now. Whenever we are tempted to think 'why don't they just...' it may be helpful to pause and consider 'what are they up against?'

Taking external conditions into consideration may provide context and perspective:

- Given the severe economic pressures out there, I'll bear with a sticky situation at work for a bit longer while I consider and explore my options.

- Could our team get together – over and above official measures – to decide how best to deal with the unavoidable consequences of the business and political outlook?

Of course, there is a distinction between externally imposed hardships we must hope are temporary on the one hand and on the other hand conditions unrelated to external pressures. It is vital to know the difference between 'the situation is externally caused' and 'the situation is caused by someone internally who could have made a different decision' as that difference influences our resilience and willingness to cope.

An attitude of gratitude

We have experienced how powerful it can be to be deliberate about appreciating one's good fortune in having the opportunity to work and grow as a professional. Harking back to the points made in Chapters 3 and 8, we use these suggested thoughts as examples of ways to frame your work situation positively:

> I am grateful to have the opportunity to be active in my profession. I will always strive to find work in an environment where my work personality is a good fit with the employing organization's culture.

> I appreciate the way every day offers me a chance to discover and learn something new to enhance my ability to serve my clients.

> It is a privilege to work in an environment where colleagues may share their expertise.

> It is deeply satisfying to be able to apply my education and qualifications to the people my organization serves and to the projects we undertake.

> I bring my enthusiasm and my dedication to work every day, hoping it will make a difference for my colleagues.

> I take with equanimity the occasional bumps in the road at work... none are insurmountable.

> In discussions, I always preface my comments with something like 'in the interest of meeting the departmental goals' or 'to meet the objectives set out in the business plan' so as to stress the fact that we are working as a team to achieve certain targets. In reality, nothing is personal – it's all about how we can collaborate to contribute to the common purpose why we are here.

> When differences of opinion arise, I seek to understand by asking questions... giving everyone a chance to explain his or her view.

I believe that no one makes it his or her business to annoy me personally... so when I feel annoyed or frustrated, I ask non-personal questions to understand: 'Could you give me more detail to help me understand how the suggested approach will play out to help us meet the deadline?'

A positive atmosphere is everyone's responsibility

Managers are expected to provide appropriate work conditions for their teams to perform. In addition, there are many ways in which we as team members can have a beneficial effect on the work environment. Ulla calls it 'bringing flowers to work' when we offer support to colleagues under stress, compliment them when they have done something well, and show an interest in them as persons. Being compassionate and accommodating – within reason – costs nothing, just as a smile and an upbeat demeanor are free:

That was one amazing presentation you just gave – where did you learn how to do it so well?

It is not lost on us how much effort you devote to helping the team succeed.

Thank you so much for supporting my proposal in the meeting – your input was just perfect!

Did you know how much we all look forward to our weekly meetings because of the energy you bring to it?

Can I do something for you in return for the help you gave me?

Dealing with difficult people

Elsewhere in the book we have touched on challenges associated with managing 'up' and 'down'. Unique difficulties are attached to dealing with colleagues who – for reasons we may never have the opportunity to understand – are negative, confrontational, passive aggressive, or otherwise unpleasant in the way they behave. (Frankly, we consider such behavior unprofessional.)

Just as we have all had the pleasure and privilege of working with delightful colleagues, we have all encountered the typical characters who can make an otherwise interesting and appealing job quite stressful: the naysayers who reject every suggestion; the envious ones who belittle others' accomplishments; the slackers who leave work for others to pick up; the gossipers who seem to take pleasure in making some co-workers feel ostracized; the critics who nitpick ad nauseam; and the moody types whose erratic manners leave others permanently worried they might be the next target of a sarcastic remark.

In outright cases of harassment, there are options for resolution. When untoward behavior is less obviously actionable, the victims are left to fend for themselves while they suffer the emotional consequences of feeling constantly stressed at work.

What can you do if you are on the receiving end of, or witness, unprofessional behavior? Options include:

- confronting the offender directly, in the hearing of witnesses, with a calm but firm 'excuse me, I believe that comment was uncalled for, and I expect an apology' or 'you may not be aware how hurtful it is when you... and I ask that you cease'

- requesting a private meeting in which you explain that you wish to point out how certain aspects of the offender's behavior are having a negative effect and how you have suggestions for other ways to act (we realize that in some cases such a course of action could make things worse, so perhaps it is best to talk the option over with a trusted colleague in advance)

- discussing the matter with colleagues who may know the offender for longer and who therefore may have advice to offer

- meeting privately with the supervisor – where possible, in the presence of a human resource representative – to describe the problematic behavior and its effect; again, there could be a perception of risk... but what if the supervisor said 'I did not realize, allow me to investigate'?

The key is to keep the focus on the consequences for the team or department rather than on your person. Remember, it is the manager's responsibility to foster a fair and productive work environment!

'But I hate my work'

Although we believe that you should remain positive, we acknowledge that there will be times when you will say 'I hate my work' and truly mean it. We have seen situations – close up and from afar – where a person's work environment has been intolerable. In some instances, the entire organization has been toxic, while in others it has been the manager who has created a caustic environment. In some cases, the work itself is not what you envisioned and the organization has no way of making it better.

One colleague was recruited by an organization and went through several rounds of interviews. He was told what the position would be and was promised a specific level of authority. After being hired, he found out the employer was not going to live up to the promises, so he quit. That decision was a painful one, but he felt it was necessary. He also believed that he would be able to explain the short tenure in that organization adequately to future employers without sounding too negative.

Another colleague found herself in a stressful situation where people yelled, deadlines constantly changed, the structure was unstable, and no one was happy. She decided to use her non-work hours to develop a new resume, research different job opportunities, gather information, and create a plan. Because she was unable financially to leave her position without having a new job lined up, she stayed in this stressful situation for nearly a year before she was able to put her plan into action. During that year, she continued to give her all at work, not wanting anyone to realize that she was considering quitting or find reasons to fire her.

Should you quit?

You may look at your situation and wonder if you should quit, especially if every avenue for amelioration of an unhealthy environment at work has been exhausted. If you believe that the situation is too toxic, leaving it is not an admission of failure but rather an act of self-preservation. It is better to remove yourself from a job that is destroying your spirit than to stay and suffer the consequences.

Obviously, it would be ideal to line up new employment before resigning, but do consider the psychic cost of dealing with the stress in the current job *and* presenting oneself positively to a potential new employer. Although it is possible – and often necessary – to look for a new job while being stressed by your current position, it can be a relief to leave the current position and ensure that you are in good spirits while looking for a new one. It is always a good strategy to have 6–12 months of financial savings to rely on between jobs.

If the tenure has not been very long in the position, one concern could be that it is necessary to stick it out for a minimum length of time (one to two years) so as not to raise flags in the resume. Again, there are ways to provide clarifying information to resume readers while avoiding negative insinuations about a past employer. One option is to state: 'I left the position in order to pursue opportunities with upward mobility.'

In future job interviews, be ready for questions about any job you held for a very short time. Practice your answer so that it is truthful without being overly negative. Keep in mind the possibility that the interviewer may know – and respect – individuals in the organization you left.

The bottom line: trust your gut

Trust your instincts. If you find yourself in a bad situation that isn't getting any better, gather information and review the facts, then decide if there are ways of surviving and thriving there. If so, then put your energy into making it work. If your gut tells you the place is killing your soul, look at your finances and decide if you want to get out of the situation immediately or if you need to wait. Whatever you do, begin immediately to plan for your future, even if that planning must happen in secret.

Finally, after you have walked out the door and counted yourself lucky to have survived, take time to consider the lessons learned. Yes, we may all learn lessons from negative situations. Often they will teach us about ourselves as well as different work environments. You might for example realize there were questions you should have asked during your job interview, during a promotion, or when meeting a new boss. Whatever the lessons are, internalize them and remember them for the future.

12

About the money

It would be wonderful to live on the *Enterprise* (the space craft of the programme *Star Trek*), where no one seems concerned about money. But we don't! Although we should enjoy our jobs, we work in order to be paid so we can afford the life we live outside our work environment.

What are you worth?

When Jill went on her first job interview, she was asked what she thought she was worth. All she knew was what her salary might be if she went to work for the federal government. Jill had no idea what her salary might be if she worked for a corporation. The interviewer told her she was worth more than she realized, and the offer Jill received proved it to be true.

How do you know what your market value is – in other words, your salary potential? If you are just graduating from a university, its office of career services should have access to employer surveys and information from recent graduates providing useful data. Since the job outlook changes from year to year, the information is only a guide.

What if you are already out in the workforce? How do you know what your worth is? Many professional associations and industry publications gather and publish salary information yearly for the use of human resource departments, hiring managers, and people like you. Median and mean salary information for specific job titles and geographic regions can often be found in industry publications. If the information was gathered by a professional association, more detailed information may be available for a fee. Although you may not want to pay for salary information, having it will put you in a better negotiating position because you will have at least the same and potentially better information than the organization with which you are negotiating has.

Within your organization there may be specific salary ranges corresponding to different levels. For example, the salary range for a supervisor and the salary range for a manager will differ according to the job responsibilities, and the ranges should not be a mystery even though they may not be considered public information. The human resources department should be able to tell you the ranges and answer any questions you have. If information on how salaries are calculated is kept hidden, consider it a license to try to negotiate what you deem to be the salary you want.

What is in a compensation package?

We tend to think of our pay as being our salary, but it involves much more. Your compensation package includes your salary, bonus options, and benefits. (Benefits are discussed in the next section.)

Your salary is what you are guaranteed to be paid as an employee for a specific time period. Salary is quoted in an amount per year; however, you should calculate how much you will receive per week or month, since that is how you will receive your income. A salary is the gross amount you will be paid, and your take home income is that amount less taxes. If you do not know what the tax rate is, check with your government and then calculate how much of your pay will go to taxes. The remaining income is what you have available for living expenses including rent or mortgage, car, food, utilities, clothing, entertainment, and so on. If you have a household budget detailing all your expenses, then it will be easy to see if your income will cover them. If you do not have a fully developed household budget, make a list of your expenses – estimating when necessary – in order to know if a given salary is enough for you to live on.

A salary figure may sound wonderful until you begin to calculate how much of it will go toward your normal living expenses. You will want to save some of your money for your future (for example, vacations, retirement) as well as for any emergencies (for example, illness, leaky roof, major car repair). In fact, conventional wisdom is that you always set aside money in a savings account from each paycheck. How much should you save? As much as possible! Even one dollar (or one pound or one franc) per day will add up. If you can set aside 5–10% of every paycheck, that would put you on a good path for the future.

Although your salary is a fixed amount, you may also receive two variable components in your compensation package: performance bonus and stock options. A performance bonus is given if your work meets a specific standard. For example, you might receive a bonus if you complete a major project ahead of schedule. Sometimes you will be told in advance that a bonus is possible and what the criteria are, so you can work toward receiving it. In other instances, the bonus may be a surprise. Bonuses are generally cash, but they may take the form of a gift of some sort (say, an appliance or a trip). Your possibility of receiving a bonus may vary from year to year, as may the organization's ability to give them.

Stock options are issued by a company allowing the receiver to buy stock in the company at a set price (often a bargain price) during a specified period of time. Note that you must exercise the stock options by purchasing the stock. In other words, you must spend money in order to acquire the stock; then you can sell the stock (at a higher price than you paid) and thus realize a gain. However, there is no guarantee that you will be able to afford to use the stock options and no guarantee that you will be able to sell the stock for a good profit. Stock options are more common for senior executives than they are for 'regular' employees.

Finally, in some cases, your compensation may include ownership of actual stock in the company. Such an arrangement may be more common in start-up companies. The idea is that if you own a piece of the company, you will be more invested in ensuring the company does well. If you do receive stock, be sure to understand any limitations placed on selling the stock as well as the impact on your income taxes.

What is in a benefits package?

For some, the benefits package is as important as, or even more important than, the salary. The benefits package includes expenses the employer is willing to pay on your behalf either in part or in full, including:

- health, dental, and eye care insurance
- education assistance including conference attendance
- child daycare
- elder care
- sick leave

- parental leave (formerly known as maternity leave)
- vacation and personal days
- retirement savings.

Every organization's benefits package is different, reflecting the value placed on keeping employees. For example, an organization whose executives believe it can easily replace its employees may offer very few benefits.

It is important to know which benefits are most important to you. At each stage in your life, different benefits will be more important. For example, a young professional may be less concerned about health insurance than someone older is.

Be sure to understand whether you need to contribute to the cost of any of the benefits. Your employer may pay most of the costs associated with health, dental, and eye care, but may expect you to contribute toward some of the costs. Those costs come out of your salary.

There are two approaches to sick leave, vacation, and 'personal days'. First, an organization may allow you to take a specific number of days away from work under these categories without pay – and without risk of losing your job. Second, an organization may allow you to take a specific number of days away from work for sick, vacation, or personal time and pay you for those days. Although it is good to have a number of days you can take off from work regardless of the circumstances, it is better to be paid for your time off.

Finally, there are government rules in some countries about mandatory benefits for employees. For example, employees in France are guaranteed 30 days of vacation, while employees in the United States are not guaranteed any at all. If your organization has locations around the world, it may have a better benefits package worldwide because of the rules in various countries and its desire to treat everyone equitably.

When benefits are more important than money

The last year Jill was in graduate school, she had an emergency root canal. Because she did not have a good insurance plan at the time, the dentist told her to wait until she was employed and had good insurance before having a crown put on the tooth because of the expense. Later that year, she was pleased to see that her job offer included medical benefits and that she was going to be able to afford the needed dental work.

Benefits are important to everyone, but they can be critically important to some. For example, people with health issues will look for an employer with good health benefits. For others, specific benefits are more important during certain phases of their careers. Keep your needs in mind when you are negotiating a job offer or a change in salary and benefits.

How to assess a job offer and negotiate your compensation

Every job offer has several components to it, including:

- job title
- duties and responsibilities
- reporting relationship
- compensation
- benefits.

Understand one thing: everything is negotiable. Everything. However, it may not be a winning strategy to negotiate every aspect of the offer. That could mark you as someone who is satisfied by nothing, a characteristic your future employer may not appreciate. You may want to select only such aspects as are most important to you and negotiate them, if necessary.

Job title, duties, and responsibilities all go together. Your job title will convey what you do (supervisor, manager, analyst) – but does it adequately communicate your responsibilities and authority? Are your responsibilities appropriate for your job title? You don't want to be supervising others and have a job title that does not convey the responsibility. Conversely, you don't want to have a job title sounding like a mid-level manager if you have secretarial responsibilities. If your job title and duties are not in alignment, bring your concern to your manager (or hiring supervisor) along with suggestions on possible changes. If necessary, gather information on appropriate job titles and duties from job search sites, survey data, or colleagues in similar positions.

Where you report within the organization conveys the importance of your work and may impact what you do. Unfortunately, reporting relationships are not always logical, since those in management positions may be trying to grab territory and build empires. Still, you should report to someone who understands and values your work. Here you may need tact and skill to inquire about the logic behind a reporting relationship that does not seem beneficial. You might ask how the reporting relationship will impact your ability to provide services to the organization and your access to budget. Caution: if you decide to suggest a different reporting relationship, do so only after you understand the politics of the organization.

No matter what you are negotiating, your goal is to get to 'yes' – as in yes, the employer will agree to your terms. You may find that a compromise is needed to provide a win–win situation. No matter what, understand that you may lose the negotiation, which means the status quo will remain. Although you may be tempted to give an ultimatum ('I won't work here unless...'), only do so if you are prepared to live up to the ultimatum. Remain calm; ultimatums generally appear when we become angry and irrational.

There is a strong possibility we may feel discouraged because the (potential) employer does not place the same value on us as we do. If you find yourself feeling depressed over the situation, take the initiative to change it. In the case of a job offer, continue to seek other offers, if possible, until you find one to your liking. In the case of a performance or salary review, consider whether it is time to begin your job search and seek another employer. Yes, finding a new job may take time; but if your current situation is depressing you, you should find the time to look for a better situation.

At one point in her career, Jill was handed information about her pay raise that didn't seem quite right. During her bus ride home, she took out a calculator and saw that the pay raise was so small as to almost be non-existent. In the winter darkness, the other riders could not see her tears. Although she was promised that a larger raise would be forthcoming the next year, Jill took it as a sign it was time to move on. Developing a plan and implementing it, however, took nearly a year... time she believes was well invested.

The salary roller coaster

We grow up believing the amount of money we earn should continue to increase year after year. In reality, our salaries increase, decrease, and stay unchanged based on the financial health of our employers. Although less than satisfactory performance could cause your salary to decrease, it is important to be aware that most salary stagnation is not related to our performance. Therefore, if you find that your salary is stalled, ask yourself these questions:

- What is the financial health of the employer?
- Can the organization, in truth, afford to increase salaries?
- Are similar organizations increasing salaries for their employees?
- Can you survive financially if your salary does not increase?
- Can you find a new employer who would pay you more in salary?

Once you have the answers, it will be up to you decide what to do. Consider your decision's impact on your future over the long term.

Trade or labor unions

In the 19th and 20th centuries unions played an important role in ensuring fair wages and safe work conditions in many industrialized nations. Unions are still important today in some industries and countries, but their importance is fading in other areas.

An institution employing unionized workers will generally operate using one of these models:

- A closed shop (or a pre-entry closed shop) employs only people who are already union members.
- A union shop (or a post-entry closed shop) will hire non-union workers but will demand that they join the union in order to stay employed.

- An agency shop requires non-union workers to pay a fee to the union for its services in negotiating their contract.

- An open shop does not require union membership in employing or keeping workers. Where a union is active, workers who do not contribute to a union still benefit from the collective bargaining process.

In some institutions, information workers belong to unions. Generally those covered by unions are paraprofessionals, but professionals may also find themselves under the protection of a union. No matter which model the institution is using, a union is there to help you. Be sure to read the union contract and understand how it impacts your work and salary. If you interview for a position in an organization with a union, do research on it, and know in advance how it will affect you.

The biggest impact of a union comes from its regulations on your salary. The union contract will mandate the conditions under which you can receive a pay increase and how large the increase might be. For example, a contract might mandate pay increases of a specific percentage each year no matter what the financial standing of the institution. Although that is a positive, the negative could be that your boss is unable to grant you a pay increase larger than what the contract mandates, even though you might deserve it.

Other professional organizations

No matter what work you do or where you work, there is a professional organization – or association – to which you can belong. These associations of like minded individuals provide excellent networking and continuous learning opportunities. If you work alone or have few colleagues in your institution, a professional association will provide the camaraderie, advice, and other social benefits you may not receive internally.

Your professional association can help you improve your salary and work conditions if it surveys its members regularly and then publishes findings on salaries and other aspects of members' work. That salary information can be useful as you negotiate a contract or pay increase with your employer. Use the information to demonstrate what other information professionals who do work similar to yours are being paid. What you hope is that your employer will want to match the documented salary in order to keep you, rather than having to recruit to fill the position if you leave.

Some employers are wise and will obtain a copy of salary surveys to use when they are considering pay increases. If your employer does so, obtain a copy of the salary survey – even if you have to order your own copy – so you have the same information. You cannot negotiate well if you lack facts.

In the end, it's not about the money

When we talk about work, we always think about the money. Are we getting paid enough? Are we getting compensation comparable to that of our colleagues? However, if you are making a living wage and are able to save money for your goals (be they retirement, vacations, a home), then money becomes less important. Indeed, people who leave their place of employment in order to work someplace else generally do so for reasons other than money – factors such as work conditions or the opportunity to enhance quality of life outside work may play a role.

At some point in your career you may even find that you will take a job – or stay in a job – because of its environment, challenges, or camaraderie. Even then, you must pay attention to what you are being paid; although you may not mind being underpaid, you do not want to set an untoward precedent for how the organization pays others.

Measuring your success

Finally, keep in mind the saying, 'Success is doing what you love. Success is loving what you do.' Know how you want to measure your success in ways other than by the amount of money you earn. You might measure your success by your position in your organization or industry, by the number of articles you have published or presentations you have given, or even by the quality of your vacations. When you go through times when the money doesn't seem to be enough, or times when work is very stressful, knowing how you are measuring your success will help keep you grounded.

13

Passing it on: collegial support or mentoring

Passing on knowledge and skills to others

Jill's friends

I have a friend who says he will donate great sums of money once he becomes rich. Until then, he will hold on to his money, supposedly spending it wisely and saving some for a rainy day. I have another friend who barely has enough money, yet is always willing to help. She would consider going without a necessity if it meant someone else's condition improved.

Like the second person, I believe 'passing it on' isn't something to be done once you have 'made it'. Rather it is something everyone should do from the beginning. You might have the impression that passing one's insight on means doing something big, but being supportive of others in reality means doing small things and doing them frequently. When I was a new corporate employee at the age of 26, my colleagues taught me the skills that helped me survive and thrive, and those skills have continued to be important. No one learns how to navigate a corporate hierarchy, travel for business, lead a team, put together a presentation for senior management, or write a performance review until it must be done. Then, wise souls in the workplace or the social network may volunteer to show how it's done.

At this very moment, you have knowledge and skills you could be passing on to others. Who are those 'others'? If you just graduated, the others are those still in school. If you have been in your position for a while, the others are those just being hired. If you are in the middle of your career, the others are those with only a few years of work behind them. Sometimes the others are people going through a career change, no matter their age, with a need for help from colleagues who have made a similar change or from colleagues in the new career field.

What is meant by mentoring?

Mentoring happens when someone who has 'been there and done that' shares experience, knowledge, or wisdom with someone less experienced. A mentor might be called an adviser, coach, guide – or just a wise person. In fact, most mentors likely just see themselves as being helpful and do not think of their assistance to others as being worthy of a formal label. They are simply sharing what they know will be helpful to another. The person being mentored, usually called a mentee (for lack of a more elegant term!) or protégé, might view the mentor as providing on the job training or just supplying helpful hints. Since mentoring can be carried out informally as well as formally, the mentor and mentee may not even recognize they are engaged in something significant. What they are doing might seem to be part of normal life. In fact, mentoring is so common that it is happening all around you right now.

Mentoring moments

You may have the impression that mentoring is a serious, formal activity. Let us dispel that idea by showing you how it may be done in small portions:

- After a webinar, an attendee sends an email to the instructor and outlines a concern in her current job. A phone call ensues in which the attendee receives expert input on the matter at hand.

- A student requests advice from a professional in the field on a choice to be made regarding employment. The matter is discussed over a coffee.

- A colleague is considering a major professional change. The local coffee shop is the venue for an in-depth discussion of options with a trusted colleague.

- For a consulting proposal, a colleague wonders about the rates to quote. Emails and phone calls take place with a seasoned consultant to assist in arriving at rates that are fair yet competitive.

- In struggling to prepare a business case for funding a major new content license or document management system, an information professional reaches out for help with structuring the arguments to be made in the case. A colleague who has been through the experience several times responds with advice.

- A student has landed an interview for a dream job but feels unprepared. A meeting with a mentor provides the venue for offering tips on answers to likely questions, ways to deflect concerns about her lack of work experience, and the appropriate outfit to wear for the particular organizational environment.

- Out of the blue, a mid-career colleague has been laid off and asks for help getting job seeking tools ready. Colleagues and members of the social network review his resume and suggest ways to parlay skills into a 'step up' rather than a 'same as before' position.

- Someone in the professional association is unsure about running for office or taking on a role as committee chair. Trusted peers encourage her, citing their own experiences holding association posts.

- A group of students is interested in exploring career opportunities. A panel of professionals with unusual jobs is staged so the students can hear about career options and opportunities.

- A colleague has experienced a painful event in the workplace and reaches out for help. A friend responds with views and insights to help assess the options.

What characterizes a mentor?

Although a mentor may teach, he or she may also be someone who listens and provides a safe space for talking through opportunities, problems, challenges, and changes. Many can share experiences, knowledge, and wisdom, but being a good impartial listener is a skill not everyone has. The people in your life who act as a sounding board are worth their weight in gold.

A mentor is someone who voluntarily and freely enters into a formal or informal relationship with another person (the mentee) in order to offer suggestions and guidance. Mentors are caring and responsible individuals but are not therapists or life coaches. A mentor may be someone in the mentee's organization or someone in a different organization, industry, or geographic region. What is important is that the mentor and mentee are able to communicate openly and experience the relationship as supportive, helpful, and free of stress.

Mentors often report how they benefit from the mentoring relationship. Some say explaining aspects of the profession gives them a better understanding of it. Others gain personal satisfaction from providing collegial support and from watching their mentees grow professionally. Many note how they acquire a fresh perspective of the profession from their mentees – a perspective they would have missed otherwise.

What characterizes a mentee?

A mentee or protégé is someone wanting to learn from or interact with a person who has more experience or knowledge about the profession or about aspects of a job. Although mentees are receivers of knowledge, they often help the mentors understand what new members of the profession are doing and thinking.

Mentees report how the mentoring relationship teaches them ideas and insights that were not taught in school. In addition, some report gaining a better understanding of their organization or industry. Most mentees say they acquire guidance that helps them perform their jobs better.

A given individual could occupy both roles. For example, a highly experienced technical expert who knows everything there is to know about a particular software suite and acts as the go-to person for any questions about it could be learning about leadership and meeting facilitation techniques from a colleague.

When a younger professional acts as a resource for a more seasoned one, we call it 'reverse mentoring'. No matter how experienced we may get, we can never say we need not learn any more. A mentee may provide the mentor with new information and skills, which makes the mentoring relationship a two-way street. An example is that younger professionals sometimes trade their skills in new technology tools for insights and advice about managerial or strategic matters from more seasoned professionals.

Mentoring activities

Once you have connected with someone in a mentoring relationship, consider engaging in a range of activities together. For example:

- Attend a relevant meeting, workshop or conference together. Afterwards discuss and reflect on the event, what occurred, what was learned, and so on.

- Go to breakfast or lunch together either as a mentoring meeting or for fun.

- Discuss the projects you each have worked on and the lessons you learned.

- Share your resumes and talk about how your different positions have supported your career goals.

- Share tips on professional reading (books, blogs, website, journals).

- Co-author an article on a topic of mutual interest.

- Attend a non-work event together, such as an art opening, to help you get to know each other better and make your conversations richer.

- Read and discuss a book, article or blog.

- Jointly conduct an information interview with a third information professional in person or as a conference call.

- Tour each other's work sites.

Note that some of these activities require you to be in the same location for the activity to occur, while other activities can be accomplished even if you are miles apart. Of course, there are many other activities you could engage in, so do not limit the possibilities. Choose activities you both see as beneficial.

How do mentors and mentees find each other?

Meetings and conferences, work relationships, and occasionally chance encounters are common means for the parties to connect. Sometimes the relationship starts out as a social connection and later evolves into an exchange of professional information. There may not be any overt or official handshake that 'from now on, we are mentor–mentee'; rather the connection simply evolves naturally. What is important is that the parties agree to enter the relationship voluntarily. They may meet in person, by phone, via email, or through social media. Some may decide to meet regularly, say twice monthly, while others interact more sporadically. Some professional associations will match mentees with mentors. When that occurs, there may be expectations about the frequency of meetings and reporting of progress. Mentoring relationships may last for a few weeks or months, others may go on for years. Very long-standing mentoring relationships may evolve into peer relationships as the mentee gains experience; in such cases, the mentoring evolves into comfortable conversations between peers.

Where do you start? Just go ahead!

You may doubt your ability to share, believing you don't have a surplus of knowledge to pass on – but that is not true. Once you reach out, you will discover how much knowledge you do have for the benefit of others. If the 'm' word sounds a little too formal to you, don't use it – just offer to help: 'I could take a look at your resume' or 'let me show you that spreadsheet trick' may be all that is needed.

It is important to keep in mind that mentoring relationships, like most other relationships, have a beginning and end – and won't necessarily be perfect. If you find your mentoring relationship to be unsatisfying, you should talk to your mentoring partner about how the relationship could be changed for the better. If the relationship remains non-beneficial, then it is perfectly acceptable to end it gracefully and seek a new one. It is important that the relationship be nurturing, helpful, and comfortable. If it is not, you are not receiving the benefits you deserve – and that holds true whether you are the mentor or the mentee.

We hope you are intrigued about the idea of passing on your knowledge and find many ways of doing it. We have found being a formal and informal mentor to be rewarding and pleasurable. It's rewarding to see someone blossom and grow, and the activities – like meeting over lunch or collaborating on a presentation – are fun.

Ready? Go!

The mentor in me: Jill

Truth be told, I do not consider myself a mentor. The word conjures up images of an old sage and I consider myself neither old nor as wise as a sage. Yet I know things and

---

What about a coach?

Professional career and personal coaches are available for hire. They can help you find a career path and improve aspects of your work life, but they cannot give you insights into your organization or industry. They likely cannot give you specific ideas or lessons to impact your career immediately in the same way an information professional mentor can.

If you feel you need someone to help identify work related or personal areas for development, then you may want to engage a *personal* coach. If you want someone to help you with job search strategies, assist you in constructing an effective resume, or unearth job openings, then you may want to engage a *career* coach. Like a sports team coach, your coach may be direct and perhaps a bit pushy in order to move you forward – that's what he or she is paid to do.

---

people others could benefit from knowing. I believe my real gift is in connecting people. I frequently find myself saying 'do you know' or 'you should know' followed by a person's name. The saying is 'it's not what you know, but who you know' and I believe in increasing the number of people my friends and colleagues know.

With social media, connecting people happens outside face-to-face conversations or the forwarding of someone's business card. It happens through sites such as LinkedIn, Facebook, and Twitter where I can quickly connect people and tell them why they need to know each other – whether they later make contact with each other is up to them. Social media make it easier to connect people who may not be in the same industry or social circles. One colleague – do I dare use the word mentee? – has said that my willingness to make these connections is rare and went on to say how helpful it was.

For me, it is important in making introductions that I trust each party will act respectfully and professionally. My reputation is at stake, and I don't want it harmed because someone might act in an untoward manner.

So here's my challenge for you: take a moment and look around you virtually. Can you find two people in your network who have something in common? Maybe they are attending the same school or conference, investigating similar technology, working in the same organization, interested in the same career path... or in some other way share an interest that is publicly known. Could there be a benefit in them knowing each other or just knowing about each other? If the answer is 'yes', then make the introduction. The introduction does not have to be long, but it does need to be clear. 'Hi... as you are both involved in... I thought you might want to know about each other...'. Then look to do another... and another... and another. Soon it will be second nature.

The mentor in me: Ulla

It all came naturally. Through my career I have had the privilege of offering countless colleagues my caring, guidance, and on-call assistance. In direct reporting relationships, I had the opportunity to coach a team member in a particular task or skill; with other colleagues, I discussed many a workplace challenge and offered ideas about new ways to look at a situation. I have been incredibly proud when colleagues thanked me for opening the door to new ideas, suggesting new ways to handle a sticky situation, describing techniques for dealing with organizational politics, sharing a structure for complex reports, and so on.

The most public and straightforward aspect of my mentoring activities is my long standing and permanent offer to review and edit resumes, coupled with presentations on the principles for constructing effective ones. Less well known publicly are my confidential discussions with colleagues seeking input on a particular professional or career related matter, but in every public presentation I stress that 'my mailbox is always open'.

How did I evolve into a natural mentor? Just as a pearl grows from a grain of sand, the evolution went something like this.

At first, I offered bend-over-backwards customer service, laying the groundwork for what I later came to identify as my brand: 'No one goes in vain to Ulla.' Over time, as I interacted with customers not just in technical but also in sales contexts, discussing the best strategies for them to advance the business case for a purchase 'upstairs', the customers formed the impression that 'Ulla usually has some useful comments to make.'

Then, teaching at local educational institutions and being active in the Special Library Association added to the perception my colleagues had – and still have – of me as an approachable person generous with her time. Over the years, word of mouth has cemented my unofficial role as someone who has been everywhere and seen everything.

Finally, writing articles and blog posts on matters of professional interest adds to the image I am still burnishing: Ulla may not have the silver bullet solution to every challenge… but she has a whole lot of insight to offer!

The bottom line for me as a colleague for my fellow professionals and students is that *I have the time of day for anyone who seeks my help.* Yes, I will ask students to recast their resumes according to my published advice before submitting them to me… but I will never turn anyone away. All I ask is 'one day, do for someone else what I have done for you'.

The unmentorables

Every mentor may encounter someone who is unmentorable. Unmentorables are people who want to be mentored – or need to be mentored – but who ignore advice, state why the advice offered won't work for them, or want to do everything their way (or not at all). They have a problem with every piece of advice that they are given. If you are mentoring a person who turns out to be unmentorable, what should you do?

If you are a formal mentor, you should talk with the individual in question about what is happening. Explain that you cannot mentor a person who does not want to be mentored. The two of you may decide to continue in the mentoring relationship in order to give the person a second chance, or decide to end the mentoring relationship. Do not feel guilty if the relationship ends; you gave it your best.

If you are an informal mentor, it could be that the individual in question does not recognize what you are trying to do. You may want to explain what you are trying to accomplish and explain what you see as resistance. Your mentee may have no idea what he or she has been doing and may indeed become more open to advice. You might also decide to just end the unsuccessful mentoring without any explanation, given how the mentee appears to be unaware of the mentoring being offered. Either decision is valid. No matter what, it is important for you to understand that some people simply cannot be mentored.

Mentoring gone wrong: Jill relates

Mentees may enter into a mentoring relationship hoping it will solve every career problem. The person may have followed an unintended career path and may want the mentor magically to create a new path. That describes one of my mentees, assigned to me by a professional association. The person had graduated with a Master's degree, but then decided to follow an unrelated career path. Although successful, the person now wanted to move into a job that would use the degree. Great! The problem was a resistance to hearing about the steps needed in order to make the change. 'Why should I have to do that?' I, the mentor, couldn't get the mentee to accept that changing career paths would require specific steps.

Soon what could have been a good relationship turned into infrequent communication and then to no communication. Mentoring only works when the mentor and mentee are knocking down barriers, not creating them. Here the barriers were the lack of ability to have open communication as well as the mentee suspecting the mentor was steering in the wrong direction.

What should have been done differently? First, the mentor and mentee should have had a longer conversation upfront. Such a conversation may have surfaced the fact that the mentee wanted advice to fit an existing mental model and not necessarily the advice the mentor shared. Second, they should have discussed specific expectations or goals, such as 'I will research job descriptions and understand what skills a successful candidate needs'. That specific activity would have proved to the mentee what experiences and skills were needed, thus backing up the mentor's advice.

Most importantly, at the beginning of the relationship, they should have discussed guidelines for ending it. We are generally uncomfortable with talking about how a relationship will end because we hope that a relationship of any kind will last a long time. Especially in formal mentoring relationships, it is important to talk about the end. Under what circumstances can a mentoring relationship stop, and who can stop it? We stopped our relationship by ceasing all communication. What we should have done was acknowledge why the relationship wasn't working and discuss other mentoring options for the mentee. That would have provided real closure instead of the feeling that something had been left unfinished.

Although this relationship didn't work, I learned from it and hope the mentee did too. Because of it, I have built every mentoring relationship I have had since then with clearer expectations and they have been more rewarding.

See Central New York Library Resources Council at *www.clrc.org/mentoring/* for a toolkit Jill developed.

Mentoring gone right: Ulla relates

It has been pointed out to me often that I have a knack for suggesting new ways to think about a situation or challenge and for interpreting potential motivations behind, say, a colleague's puzzling actions. Many are the times I heard something along the lines, 'I am so glad I talked to you – you shed an entirely different light on what was bothering me.'

During my employment, it was my privilege to work with talented colleagues who gladly shared the secrets they had learned – and with staff members who were eager to learn from me. Once I got over the mistaken ideas I had about how a manager is supposed to act, I consciously attempted to be someone who could be trusted in a confidential chat and someone who would gladly show the ropes if a task was new to someone. I came to believe that a manager's top obligation is to support the team and create opportunities for all members to grow – in ways suited to each individual's own style of learning – and began to look for ways to create victories for my troops. I have been the unofficial word processing tutor, the public presentation coach, the sounding board when there were tensions in the office, the mock manager in a practice performance review, and so on. Rather than issuing directives (as in 'set up the report this way') I tried to give my staff members the opportunity to demonstrate their creativity (as in 'I'm thinking the key items to feature at the top are these, and maybe a table format could work well – why don't you give it a stab and we'll have a look at it tomorrow?'). I admit there were times I dreaded losing a valuable team member, but I was the proudest person in the room when he or she got a promotion away from my department and my guidance had been a key factor.

After leaving employment to consult, I have continued to aspire to the role of 'sage dispenser of suggestions', often as a natural adjunct to the resume review service I have offered for longer than I can remember. At this stage, I pray 'everyone knows' that my virtual door is permanently open, and that I'm always willing to meet over a coffee to discuss a work or career-related matter. I have lost count of how many times I met with a colleague and later heard from him or her how valuable our exchange had been. Some colleagues return from time to time for more advice and I take that as evidence they appreciate what I offer!

14

Our colleagues speak: career snapshots

The following pages are the result of interviews conducted with colleagues whose points of view we wanted to include. We felt they would offer inspiration for readers, and we are grateful to our colleagues for sharing their experience.

Thanks to Elaine P. Patton, MSLIS G'11, Syracuse University, for her assistance on this chapter.

Constance Ard

Constance Ard is a business analyst and consultant offering extensive research and content management skills to her clients. Typical projects include in-depth analysis of web search capabilities for non-profits, preparation and training on social media in the legal environment, and content analysis for a new web presence. Constance is an active information professional organization volunteer, having served as chair of the Legal Division of the Special Libraries Association (SLA) and chair of the Kentucky Virtual Library Advisory Committee. In October 2009 Constance completed her first book, *Next Generation Corporate Libraries and Information Services*. In October 2008 she was presented with the Professional Award by the Kentucky Chapter of the

SLA. Other awards include the Kentucky Libraries Association Special Librarian of the Year Award 2007 and the Kentucky Chapter of SLA Outstanding Chapter Member Award 2006. In September 2010 Constance expanded her services through adding a partner to increase her firm's range of technical offerings.

What inspired you to enter the profession?

As with most things in my life, I entered the information profession by chance rather than plan. Having spent a semester in the Graduate History Program at the University of Kentucky, my practical nature took over. As a junior high and high school student, I had spent most of my free time with the librarians. Their influence, coupled with the fact that I was working at the campus Math Library and my need to have a practical profession, inspired me to visit the Library and Information Science Graduate School at the University of Kentucky. And the rest, as they say, is history. I do give credit to my junior and senior high school librarians for influencing me in a positive manner to see the power of libraries and the services they provide.

What has been your most significant accomplishment in your career to date?

The most significant accomplishment in my career to date is the daily ability to provide information services as an independent professional and pay my bills. Simple though that may sound, that success inspires me to keep offering great solutions to my clients.

Many significant accomplishments throughout my career have helped my clients succeed. Some are as simple as providing an updated case history for a seminal case as the attorney was finishing a filing. Others are as ambitious as offering an overall content creation and management protocol that helped a company survive the economic downturn.

Some may wonder why I don't put the publication of my book as the number one career accomplishment. I am not discounting the importance of that publication by any means. It is just that, to me, that's what I do – it is just one more well-executed project that continues to build my reputation as a capable information professional.

What career events have mattered most in your life?

Career events that have mattered most in my life include a variety of support and recognition from my colleagues. First, the election as chair-elect-elect of the SLA Legal Division in 2007 leading to my service in 2010 as chair. It was equaled by the recognition of my fellow Kentucky Chapter SLA members when they awarded me the Professional Award in 2008. The timing of this presentation was most significant, a mere four months after the launch of my independent information professional career. The recognition by these professionals gave me a much needed ego boost at a time when I wasn't sure I had made the right decision.

What learning, people, or events have stood out in your career or education?

On the job learning has been a tremendous source of education. Of course that learning could not have occurred without the mentors and colleagues who did the teaching. Lynn Fogle, one of my former supervisors, taught me a huge amount about law librarianship and organizational politics. One of my current clients also serves as an ideal mentor in the consulting world. I feel as though I am learning at the knees of the greatest guru, Stephen E. Arnold. From Stephen, I am learning client relations and how to recognize opportunities, and I'm increasing my technical skills daily.

In addition, I must recognize Ulla de Stricker who provided me the best career guidance during my transition from day job to consulting. Her wisdom and guidance offered me a much needed objective perspective on the challenges I faced in my job versus the opportunities I could embrace. Knowing that she understood and agreed with my perceptions and receiving her encouragement was a lifeline. Her mentoring has not stopped, and she continues to help me succeed with each new challenging and exciting opportunity by offering me the wisdom of her own experiences.

The wealth of mentors and colleagues I have to call on when I face a difficult situation is the secret to my own success. There are many others, not named here, who have my back.

What did you need to know in order to manage your career that you learned too late?

When to leave a bad situation!

What are you still interested in learning in terms of managing your career?

I still need to learn time management in order to have a better work–life balance. The struggles I face as an independent information professional mean meeting deadlines in order to satisfy clients for current and future projects. Oftentimes, my leisure time is scarce or nonexistent. There's always a need for specific skills but without time management, I can't fit any more learning into the day.

Who were/are the two or three top inspirational people for you and why?

The top inspirational people in my career are my mother, who promised me that if I 'got an education' I could do anything, and my partner, Cammie Sizemore, who has always had faith that I would do anything I set my mind too. Without my mother's guidance, I would not be who I am. Without Cammie's support and encouragement, I would not be doing what I love. One additional person must be mentioned: Shawn Livingston remains a constant support in my personal and professional life. He provides me exceptional research advice and served as my editorial advisor and research assistant while writing my book. In addition, he is one of my dearest friends and helps me out with that work–life balance thing.

If you had it to do over again, what would you do differently?

The single thing I would do differently is to have left my day job about 18 months earlier than I did. I struggled longer in that position than was necessary. Hindsight is 20/20. After leaving, it was easier to see that the changes I wanted were not possible within the existing organizational structure.

If you had it to do over again, what would you do the same?

I would do everything else the same. Even the mistakes I have made have been invaluable in shaping me into the professional I am today. If I had not learned from those mistakes, it would be a different story, but continuous learning from both success and failure makes for a great professional in any industry.

What advice do you have for people entering the profession or people who will be making a significant change in their careers?

Advice I would offer any professional includes a very practical piece I learned from one of my early career mentors: always keep your resume current, not only with positions but also with accomplishments. Another is to have mentors and advisors you can call on. Everyone has something to learn and offer; build your network to take those opportunities.

Speaking at a graduation, what one piece of career advice would you give?

Build your network!

Lori Bell

Lori Bell is a lecturer at the San José State University School of Library and Information Science and the former director of innovation for the Alliance Library System. She has an MSLIS from the University of Illinois and an advanced certificate in distance learning from Western Illinois University. She has worked in a variety of library settings including as director of a talking book center for the print impaired; as medical librarian for a hospital library; as director for a community college library; as director of IT for Alliance Library System; and in several public library settings as a reference librarian, children's librarian, and outreach librarian.

What inspired you to enter the profession?
I was working as a student in the government documents section of the library at Western Illinois University as an undergrad. I had a history major but did not know what I wanted to do until I worked in the library.

What has been your most significant accomplishment in your career to date?
I feel my work in Second Life and library development there has been the most significant and successful accomplishment.

What career events have mattered most in your life?
I have loved working at the Alliance Library System in a variety of positions (talking books, technology, innovation). I have worked there twice for a total of 18 years and have enjoyed it more than any other type of library position I have had. In 2004 I had the opportunity to do adjunct teaching for Dominican University and University of Illinois. In 2008 I started teaching adjunct for San José State University SLIS and I love teaching! It is exciting to work with people starting out no matter what age!

What learning, people, or events have stood out in your career or education?

In 2001 I went to Western Illinois University to earn a certificate in distance learning. In 2004 I got the certificate and began teaching online. I am so glad I got this certificate, which gave me the opportunity to teach online.

What did you need to know in order to manage your career that you learned too late?

I wish I had earned a second Master's degree early on in my career. Not having that degree has limited my opportunities in academic librarianship.

What are you still interested in learning in terms of managing your career?

I want to continue to learn library and technology skills to keep up with the profession and make myself marketable for a variety of library positions.

Who were/are the two or three top inspirational people for you and why?

Three people were inspirations for me: my dad, Loren Logsdon, is an English professor and shared with me and my siblings a love of books and reading and a love of teaching and sharing knowledge with others. He is passionate about teaching and literature and has shared that with his family and hundreds of students throughout his career.

My most recent boss, Kitty Pope, is excited and enthusiastic about the profession and that rubbed off on us as her co-workers and colleagues. She created a fun work environment and encourages us all to try new things.

I worked for my former boss, Valerie Wilford, for a total of 12 years, longer than I have worked for any boss. She gave me my first opportunity to work in a technology position, which made me realize how much I enjoy working in that area.

If you had it to do over again, what would you do differently?

I would get a second Master's early in my career.

If you had it to do over again, what would you do the same?

I would still get a library degree. I love working in the profession and have had no regrets.

What advice do you have for people entering the profession or people who will be making a significant change in their careers?

Do what you love and love what you do.

What advice are you seeking from those who have been in the information profession for a number of years?

Advice I'm seeking has to do with how to reinvent yourself or what skills are most important now in this job market – how to remain relevant in 21st century librarianship in the last half of my career.

Patrick Danowski

Patrick Danowski is a computer scientist and scientific librarian. In May 2010 he started to build up the electronic library of the Institute of Science and Technology Austria. He has worked as Emerging Technologies Librarian (Fellow) at the CERN (European Organization for Nuclear Research) Scientific Information Service. From 2006 to 2009 he worked at the Staatsbibliothek zu Berlin, where he undertook a number of different projects. In the International Federation of Library Associations and Institutions (IFLA) he founded the libraries and Web 2.0 discussion group. He trained as an academic librarian at Zentral und Landesbibliothek Berlin, while he did a Master's degree in library and information science at Humboldt University. He has been blogging since September 2006 about Library 2.0 and other themes in his weblog 'Bibliothek 2.0 und mehr' (Library 2.0 and more) and gives talks and workshops about Web 2.0 and libraries on the national and international level.

What inspired you to enter the profession?

The idea of access to information for everybody.

What has been your most significant accomplishment in your career to date?

Presentation and communication skills are essential.

What career events have mattered most in your life?

Giving a presentation at the IFLA conference was a very good experience because of the international atmosphere. Networking with lots of people helped me later to find my job at CERN.

What learning, people, or events have stood out in your career or education?

Having two weeks of personal training by Claudia Lux during my time as trainee in her library taught me a great deal about management. The opportunity to visit international conferences like European Library Automation Group (ELAG), IFLA, and Internet Librarian International was eye opening. During my time on the board of directors of Wikimedia Germany, I learned a lot about how volunteer organizations work.

What did you need to know in order to manage your career that you learned too late?

It's never too late, but I learned late about time management and networking. I'm still struggling with writing complex texts.

What are you still interested in learning in terms of managing your career?

Improving my English skills and maybe learning another language. I need to learn much more about management.

Who were/are the two or three top inspirational people for you and why?

Steve Jobs, David Weinberger, Claudia Lux, Stephen Abram, Michael Stephens, Jimmy Wales – there are so many people with cool ideas!

If you had it to do over again, what would you do differently?

Not sure if I would do something differently because I love my jobs and I love the results. But after I studied computer science I needed one year to decide to work in the library world – maybe I could have made that decision more quickly.

If you had it to do over again, what would you do the same?

Going to CERN, even if it would be only for one year, because it was such a good experience to work in an international organization. It gave me a totally different understanding of culture and allowed me to meet so many nice people.

What advice do you have for people entering the profession or people who will be making a significant change in their careers?

Change is always good but not easy – keep that in mind if things don't happen as fast as you expected. Talk to younger people to get a feeling for where change is happening – not only in technology – and always stay open to new ideas even if you don't immediately understand what is behind them. Always be proud of your job – it is something cool!

Speaking at a graduation, what one piece of career advice would you give?

Go out there and talk: talk to your colleagues, talk to other librarians, talk to the vendors, and most important talk to people outside of the field of libraries and your friends. And listen to what they have to say to pick up their opinions and the ideas they can bring into libraries.

Eli Edwards

Eli Edwards is web content consultant for an online publisher of legal information. She holds a MLIS from San José State University and a Juris Doctorate (JD) from Santa Clara University School of Law. Eli tends to put whimsical titles on her business cards, such as 'Information Bounty Hunter' and 'Info Diva'. However, she's serious about information policy, including topics such as internet speech, online privacy, media law and regulation, government transparency, and the ethics of information retrieval in a Web 2.0 world. Such topics are discussed in her blog 'Confessions of a Mad Librarian'.

What inspired you to enter the profession?

It was a series of fits and starts. I nearly lived in the school and public libraries as a kid and teen, but hadn't considered working in one. In college, I lucked into working for Los Angeles Public Library (LAPL) in technical services, going through records databases to find records LAPL could import to develop its own online catalog. I loved being there, but it was only a temp job and I didn't type fast enough to qualify for the city's civil service requirement for permanent positions.

I had developed a deep love for newspapers (Rest In Peace, *Los Angeles Herald Examiner*) and I wanted to work in newspapers and around media but not necessarily as a reporter. When I was in my late 20s, I 'crashed' a journalism conference being held at a local university and heard a heralded *L.A. Times* investigative reporter praise the news librarians who helped him with an enterprise story that shook up the county administration and eventually closed down a hospital. After the talk, I rushed into the throng of questioners and asked, 'how does one get a job in the news library at the *Times*?' His answer was simply, 'I believe they all have MLISs.'

What has been your most significant accomplishment in your career to date?

I feel I'm still working on significant accomplishments. I've worked in some great places – ironically, the two newspapers I've worked for have either eliminated their entire news research staff or shut down the paper as a whole (one of those alternative weeklies).

What career events have mattered most in your life?

The event that had gotten me the most notice, I think, was when I wrote about Stanford and the Google Books Project early on in the process. Certainly, my blog's visitor number spiked!

Going back, that college job for LAPL mentioned above – that's key. That was, for many years, my favorite job... and that's counting the time I spent as an extra in Hollywood!

What learning, people, or events have stood out in your career or education?

My internships have been key – working for a digital library, a newspaper, and a legal information provider has given me new skills and allowed me to meet really wonderful people.

I also learn a lot at conferences – not only in the people I meet, but being able to find out what other people in the profession are concerned about. Getting the big picture about an area of librarianship has been invaluable. And then, of course, there's law school. It was fun in some ways, traumatizing in others, and I'm still working on integrating the two spheres of knowledge into a productive and working whole. I'm getting there.

What did you need to know in order to manage your career that you learned too late?

Don't keep your head down too far or people will forget you are there.

What are you still interested in learning in terms of managing your career?

I am still trying to learn how to put myself 'out there' – learning how to take my skills, developed from rather diverse experiences, forward.

Who were/are the two or three top inspirational people for you and why?

Oh, there have been so many inspirational people! But one of the top ones has been Bill Fisher at San José State University. He had such a fearsome reputation among the first-year students in the library program. But he challenged me in so many great ways, and he became a mentor and a friend. Among his works, he helped me get published in the library literature, gave great advice about classes and provided a lot of support when I decided to do a thesis to fulfill graduation requirements. Also, he's a funny man.

Another is Mary Minow. The more I studied certain aspects of librarianship (library polices, intellectual freedom, digitization), the more interested I became in how the law affected libraries and how they operate. I didn't meet Mary until after I graduated from SJSU, but once we did meet, she took me under her wing. She was a strong supporter of me going to law school and, right now, I'm very pleased to work with her on our state library association's Intellectual Freedom Committee. She's whip-smart, supportive, and so very, very nice.

If you had it to do over again, what would you do differently?

I would have gone to library school sooner. I took a bit of flailing in various professions and industries (teaching, bookselling, public relations, database management) before I realized a common thread – I like working with information.

I really should have learned a programming language and a statistical package. Actually, I did both when I was quite young, but I've forgotten them completely. And it's a shame because I see a lot of great and interesting positions for non-profits and academic libraries that require those two things. I think it would make me a more powerful and effective researcher.

If you had it to do over again, what would you do the same?

I would definitely still join the Special Libraries Association (SLA), still be a part of the News Division – I have learned so much being a part of the division.

What advice do you have for people entering the profession or people who will be making a significant change in their careers?

For new people entering the profession, I would say... figure out how to integrate what you love with what you want to do with your new career. The advice I'm looking for from veterans would be the same: how does one find or create opportunities to do what one loves as part of a career?

Speaking at a graduation, what one piece of career advice would you give?

Don't be afraid to step up to the plate. If you need help, ask. If you want to work on that project, ask. If someone poses a question and you believe you have the answer, say it. If you see your hero and want to talk with them, even to say 'Hi, I love your work, may I email you?', do it. In other words, don't hide that light under a bushel.

Nicole Engard

Nicole C. Engard is the director of Open Source Education at ByWater Solutions. In addition to her daily responsibilities, Nicole has been published in several library journals and keeps the library community up to date on web technologies via her website 'What I Learned Today...' (*www.web2learning.net*). In 2007 Nicole was named one of *Library Journal's* Movers & Shakers; she edited *Library Mashups*, which was published by Information Today, Inc. in 2009; and in 2010 her book *Practical Open Source Software for Libraries* was published by Chandos.

What inspired you to enter the profession?

When I graduated with an undergraduate degree in literature and computer programming I had a very hard time deciding what I wanted to do for a living. On one hand I wanted to write books for the rest of my life and on the other I got an amazing sense of accomplishment from writing computer programs. I spread my resumes far and wide and figured I was young and could try several careers before settling on a final one. Unlike many new graduates I was extremely lucky and fell into the perfect career for me on the first try. I was hired by Jenkins Law Library in Philadelphia, PA, as a web assistant. My job description included writing content for the website and helping develop new web tools. In my six years at the library I moved from web assistant to web manager, developed at least five applications to improve librarian workflow, and wrote two full length articles on those projects. I was in a role that met both of my dreams! Five years into my career at Jenkins I decided that I wanted to know more, I wanted to understand my colleagues better, and so I went to get my MLIS at Drexel, which led me to where I am today.

What has been your most significant accomplishment in your career to date?

I think of my career as a many faceted thing. In my writing career the most significant accomplishment was writing my first solo book. In my programming career I'd have to say my most significant accomplishment was changing the way librarians at Jenkins Law Library worked by developing several applications specifically for them. And most important to me personally is the fact that I have taught hundreds, if not thousands, of librarians about technologies to improve their workflow.

What career events have mattered most in your life?

Making the decision to study library science and stay in the information science field was a defining moment for me. From then on everything else was just the logical progression. Receiving my first invitation to speak to a group of librarians, being asked to participate as a chapter author, being asked to edit an entire work, and being asked to write my first solo title; all of these things came from that one decision.

What learning, people, or events have stood out in your career or education?

In 2005 I attended the Internet Librarian Conference in Monterey, California. Many of the speakers were talking about blogging and sharing what you learned online. I left that conference and started my very own blog, aptly named 'What I Learned Today...'. If it hadn't been for those librarians sharing their knowledge with me I would never have felt comfortable enough to start my own library technology blog. That blog then led to several job offers, writing offers, and speaking offers – all of which have made my career what it is today.

What did you need to know in order to manage your career that you learned too late?

To stand up for myself and what I believe in. Too many professionals find themselves in a position where they are unhappy or feel helpless; it's important to remember that you have a choice and you matter. Knowing that led me to where I am now, in a position I love with a company that shares my ideals – but that was not something I knew right out of undergraduate school.

What are you still interested in learning in terms of managing your career?

Balance is always hard to figure out. When to say yes to an opportunity and when to turn things down is always a hard decision for me to make. I always want to say yes to everything because it seems wrong to turn down an opportunity to further my career and to educate others.

Who were/are the two or three top inspirational people for you and why?

There are so many names of people I can think of who have led me to where I am today, who have taught me things I wouldn't have learned any other way. First, when I think about how I came to choose librarianship as my final career, I think of Kathy Coon, who was the deputy director at the Jenkins Law Library when I was there. She encouraged me to think for myself, to start writing in library journals, and to go out among my colleagues and share my knowledge. When I think of people outside of the industry I of course think of my parents. They owned their own businesses for most of my childhood and taught me so much about the business world and inspired me to be whatever I wanted. Finally, I couldn't be where I am now if it weren't for Chris Cormack, who worked as one of the first developers of the Koha Integrated Library System. He nurtured my love of library technology and introduced me to the world of open source software.

If you had it to do over again, what would you do differently?

Honestly, I probably wouldn't have bothered getting my MLIS. I think that was an expense that I'm going to be paying off for years to come, and one that didn't really get me any more pay or a better job. I feel that experience is more important than a degree and I could have taken a few research classes hosted by library associations to get the same (and maybe even better) education.

If you had it to do over again, what would you do the same?

The best decision I ever made was to start my own blog. Not only would I do it again, but I'd have done it earlier in my career! It is my blog that brought me to the attention of the three employers I've had since leaving Jenkins Law Library. People read my site and saw what I was learning and thought I'd be a good addition to their companies.

What advice do you have for people entering the profession or people who will be making a significant change in their careers?

For those entering the profession or thinking about joining an information profession, be prepared to never stop learning. The world of information is being turned upside down by technology and if you're not interested in learning, then you're not going to get very far. I always tell my students that they don't have to use every bit of technology that's out there, but they do have to know that it's out there and learn about how it's being used in and out of the profession. For those who are in the profession already, I say the same thing. I hear too many stories of people who have no love for learning, people who are too busy to take a class, people who think the old ways are best. These people have lost their passion and may find that taking a professional development class can ignite that passion again simply by introducing a new tool with new possibilities.

Speaking at a graduation, what one piece of career advice would you give?

Don't rule anything out. You may think you have it all figured out, but it's surprising how your skills can be used successfully in a career you never even considered. Keep your mind and eyes open and never ever stop learning.

Sergio Felter

Starting as a typical information professional, Sergio Felter has focused on content management and new media. Now, he seeks to use social media to spread knowledge and enthusiasm for creating a better world and is active as an online ambassador, social media specialist, and networker. Favorite working quote: 'Enthusiasm is the mother of effort, and without it nothing great was ever achieved.'

What inspired you to enter the profession?

My studies naturally led me to the profession.

What has been your most significant accomplishment in your career to date?

Making a change in the profession. I always work with knowledge and I like to spread it around. Discover it, put it somewhere, share it with someone. I started by entering documents into a library system... I wanted to do more.

What career events have mattered most in your life?

I worked at the Netherlands Red Cross as a content manager, and it was positive for me to be working for humanity. It is important for people to be comfortable in sharing their knowledge. Besides documents and systems, we must care about the human side.

What learning, people, or events have stood out in your career or education?

Among those who have helped me improve myself is Ulla de Stricker and others who are very experienced and open about what they are doing. It's obvious they are eager to share what they know. Communication is paramount.

What did you need to know in order to manage your career that you learned too late?

There is a huge difference between knowledge in documents and knowledge in the heads of people – we need to make that distinction as it is essential for the result.

What are you still interested in learning in terms of managing your career?

Staying connected is essential to building our careers – we need to know a lot of people. I spend a lot of time on Twitter; when world events occur and I search the news expertly, people ask me 'how do you do it? How do you find it?'

Who were/are the two or three top inspirational people for you and why?

1. My family – father, mother, brother, sister – they are all people I admire. They are pursuing what means most to

them; for example, my sister danced in musicals and now is becoming a doctor, specializing in people who dance or make music.

2. I admire much in many people! Everyone has something special to offer – it may just take time to find out what it is!

If you had it to do over again, what would you do differently?

I might have been more willing to ask for help from other people in terms of what to do with my life.

If you had it to do over again, what would you do the same?

Don't take the easiest way to get to your goal. You have to overcome difficulties to get better. My road to success was off the beaten track, but I'm stronger for it.

What advice do you have for people entering the profession or people who will be making a significant change in their careers?

My advice is to make yourself vulnerable, accept that other people can help you. When you start, you don't have experience. If one is in the middle of a career, it may be difficult to go further, so what I would advise is getting to a higher level in information. I'm still searching for how to become better.

Speaking at a graduation, what one piece of career advice would you give?

You have to be aware... if you want to be a good info professional you must stay connected with the new technologies, because the people you are working for are also working on new things. Be a facilitator for your clients or your customers. Do your best for everybody.

Stacey Greenwell

Stacey Greenwell is Associate Dean for Academic Affairs and Research at University of Kentucky Libraries. Prior to accepting that position, she was the head of the Information Commons (the Hub) at the University of Kentucky. The Hub combines a technology help desk and computer lab with a traditional library reference desk. Active in the Special Libraries Association (SLA), she is a past chair of the Information Technology Division, the founder of the Academic Division, and a fellow of the SLA. A 2009 fellow of the Frye Leadership Institute, she presents frequently at national conferences on technology, library, and instruction topics. In addition to several publications, she writes regularly about information commons, library, and IT issues on her blog 'The Uncommon Commons'.

What inspired you to enter the profession?

I am one of those strange people who always wanted to be a librarian. At age five, I was so enamored of my local public library that I made cards and pockets for my books and checked them out to my parents. Not many kids like to play librarian, but I did.

What has been your most significant accomplishment in your career to date?

My role in developing the Information Commons at the University of Kentucky (also known as the Hub). I worked with a terrific group of people on the initial planning committee, served as the interim head, and was ultimately appointed to the permanent position. We've been open for over three years, and I love what an important, vibrant student space it is on our campus.

What career events have mattered most in your life?

Tapping into the expertise of others and collaborating with others for a common goal have been so important to me. I dearly value the leadership experience, professional contacts, and friends I have gained from my active involvement in the SLA. The Frye Institute for higher education professionals was one of the most influential and career-changing experiences I have ever had.

What learning, people, or events have stood out in your career or education?

I have worked with so many good people; I've been fortunate to have a number of mentors from public libraries at the beginning of my career to professionals from around campus now. The SLA and Frye have both been invaluable to me.

What did you need to know in order to manage your career that you learned too late?

You are the only one who can truly respect and manage your own time. It is so easy to be everyone's go to person for consultation, advice, proofreading, volunteering, venting, whatever – many of us are such helpful people by nature. If you aren't careful, there won't be any time left for you. It can be so hard to say no, but sometimes it is just necessary. Not that I have taken this advice, of course.

What are you still interested in learning in terms of managing your career?

I am a year into a doctoral program in education, focused on instructional design and technologies. I am so glad I have embarked on this path, though I now especially need to work more on learning to say no.

If you had it to do over again, what would you do differently?

I would have started my doctoral program several years ago. The coursework is so relevant and interesting, particularly for my current position. I am so excited to be involved in research that has an impact on what I do at work. I keep finding new opportunities that will be open to me with this experience and the degree.

If you had it to do over again, what would you do the same?

Take the information commons job! It was a leap for me as I had become very accustomed to my IT support role in the library. It was a rather unique position – hence my involvement with special librarians – and I was pretty comfortable there. Moving into the commons role was moving back into public service, doing more traditional library work, but also involved all the challenges of getting a new student service off the ground. It was a risk, but it has been so rewarding!

What advice do you have for people entering the profession or people who will be making a significant change in their careers?

Get involved with a professional organization! I can't stress that enough. I wasn't involved as a student, and I wish I had been. I have learned so much from the SLA, had so many leadership opportunities, and developed friendships from around the world.

Speaking at a graduation, what one piece of career advice would you give?

Network! Get involved with your professional organization! I realize that is a common theme in my responses, but so much of my leadership experience has come from my professional organization. A professional organization is a great way to get your feet wet – run a meeting, plan a program, manage a budget, etc. – these opportunities aren't always there at work, especially early in your career. Volunteering for your professional organization can give you a wealth of experience.

Michael C. Habib

Michael Habib works for Elsevier as a product manager for Scopus. Prior to this position he held roles in such varied institutions as a public library, academic libraries, a social OPAC vendor, a print-on-demand do-it-yourself publisher, and a bookstore. He received his MSLIS from the School of Information and Library Science at the University of North Carolina (UNC) at Chapel Hill in 2006 and holds a Bachelor of Arts (AB) in philosophy from Boston College. He is based in Amsterdam where he organizes social events for ex-patriots in his spare time.

What inspired you to enter the profession?

I was searching for a profession working in higher education that did not involve getting a PhD. I was also interested in a career related to the web that didn't involve being a programmer. The third element of librarianship that attracted me was the strong professional ethics related to intellectual freedom and privacy. This was in 2002–2003 when the PATRIOT Act was at the center of this debate and I was very impressed with the American Library Association's (ALA's) lobbying efforts to protect reader privacy. Furthermore, these issues were becoming increasingly important with the emergence of the web and librarianship seemed an excellent profession to gain influence over web information policy.

In addition to these topical reasons, I was very inspired by the conversations being held by librarian bloggers and on online library discussion groups. I felt I could be immediately included in the conversations of the profession. It also helped me get an idea of the people in the profession and I was inspired by their passion. I also got a technician position at a local public library and took a few classes part time through the local library school. Both of these experiences gave me an opportunity to dip my toe in the water and get an idea of whether I would like the profession.

What has been your most significant accomplishment in your career to date?

This is a very difficult question, because the answer differs depending on what aspect of my career I am discussing. My Master's paper has been widely read and has probably been my biggest contribution to the profession. In my work, I am currently very excited that a version of a prototype I created is going to be turned into a production product that serves a million users a year.

What career events have mattered most in your life?

Getting my first library job as a reference technician at a local public library was certainly the starting point of it all. Later, choosing a Master's program that suited my needs and then relocating to matriculate certainly helped set the direction for my career. While in graduate school I served as President of the Student Chapter of the ALA, which established my commitment to participating in the profession at large. Similarly, my positive experience of the first conference I attended set me on a trajectory to be a frequent speaker. Starting my blog has proved to be hugely important for my career. Similarly, choosing a topic for and writing my Master's paper helped me lay out my vision for the future and sketch out a career path for achieving this vision.

Thinking about what I wanted to do after graduate school was the next major turning point in my career. The first professional position I took was going to truly set the course for my career. I think my choice to enter the private sector has made a major difference in my perspective on what it means to be a librarian. Relocating to the Netherlands to take my current position has certainly changed my life and my outlook on the profession significantly.

What learning, people, or events have stood out in your career or education?

The library blogging community has been hugely influential in my career and education. The faculty at UNC School of Information and Library Science and the courses I took there were extremely important to my education and career.

What did you need to know in order to manage your career that you learned too late?

I needed to have a better idea of how the private sector worked and what opportunities were available there. I would have been able to focus my education and job search skills differently had I known about the options available in the wider information industry.

Who were/are the two or three top inspirational people for you and why?

As far as inspiration for the profession goes, I would have to say Michael Stephens of Tame the Web and Paul Jones of ibiblio.org, UNC. Michael's enthusiasm for the future of the profession, focus on user-centered services, and pragmatic use of technology has inspired me in many ways. It helped inspire me to start my blog, to start public speaking, and gave me the courage to forge my own path in the profession. Paul was my professor at UNC and knowing him helped connect me to the wider world of web culture beyond libraries. He also was an inspiration to forge my own path.

If you had it to do over again, what would you do differently?

I would have been more aggressive trying to create opportunities with potential employers. I think I maybe could have gotten my ideal position faster had I lobbied individual employers more actively.

If you had it to do over again, what would you do the same?

Everything! I have learned something from every experience and am where I am today because of it.

What advice do you have for people entering the profession or people who will be making a significant change in their careers?

Don't be afraid to try new things. I think there is often too much fear that it is difficult to transition between different types of library jobs and this fear holds a lot of people back. Do what you are passionate about. If you take a job at a public library, it doesn't mean you can't later transition to an academic. If you work for a vendor, it doesn't mean you can't later work in a library. And if you are a reference librarian, it doesn't mean you can't later be a cataloger. As long as you are passionate about your work, go for it and it will work out.

Speaking at a graduation, what one piece of career advice would you give?

Network both online and off. Every position I have held since finishing my MSLIS has been through my network. The best jobs always go to someone who has made a connection. Go to every conference you can afford to. Participate in conversations online. Go to local networking events. In general, you should network as much as possible. I would also advise that it is important to create a personal brand. Blog, speak, research, and write about your passion. Promote your brand. If your ideas are good, someone will hire you to implement them. If people don't know your passion, they can't recruit you.

Bruce Harpham

A recent graduate, Bruce is exploring the directions his career may take.

What inspired you to enter the profession?
After finishing a MA in history, I was uncertain where to take my career. I had worked in an archive during my undergraduate studies and at a public library in high school, so that seemed worth exploring. I applied to a library school and was admitted. It just seemed like a good fit for my skills and interests.

What has been your most significant accomplishment in your career to date?
My Master's thesis project – exploring the net neutrality debate in Canada and the United States – is the most important accomplishment thus far.

What career events have mattered most in your life?
I had the opportunity to attend three professional conferences in 2009 (Ontario Library Association, Canadian Library Association, Special Libraries Association) and those were significant events in terms of realizing the many types of work information professionals do.

What learning, people, or events have stood out in your career or education?
Stephen Abram, Ulla de Stricker, and a number of other librarians I've met locally have given much of their time to advise me in specific matters.

What did you need to know in order to manage your career that you learned too late?
During my graduate studies, I was too focused on traditional academic things like doing a thesis. In some ways, I think that was a mistake. I should have focused much more energy

on trying to acquire further work experience to enhance my resume.

What are you still interested in learning in terms of managing your career?

One of the side effects of graduate school (in any field, I believe) is to underscore how little you know and how much there is to learn. Beyond that, I feel librarians have a professional duty to stay informed about trends in media, publishing, and communications since those have such an important effect on our work. Our context is changing all the time and that's why we need to stay in learning mode. Beyond that, I'm just very dedicated to learning! I love it!

Who were/are the two or three top inspirational people for you and why?

Stephen Abram has such confidence and vision in where the profession is going and how we can make it better. I like wine expert Gary Vaynerchuk's dedication to business and practical experience in making social media work.

If you had it to do over again, what would you do differently?

I would have taken every volunteer task I could handle in local professional groups, and every job shadow and other internship I could. My resume needs more experience on it!

Ruth Kneale

Ruth Kneale is the systems librarian for the Advanced Technology Solar Telescope in Tucson, Arizona. Prior to that she was the librarian and webmaster for the Gemini Observatory in Hilo, Hawaii, and the Gemini 8m Telescopes Project (what observatories are before they grow up) in

Tucson. She is a librarian in geek clothing whose first program was created using BASIC on a TRS-80 with a tape drive. Ruth holds a Master's degree in information resources and library science from the University of Arizona and a Bachelor of Science in astronomy and physics. An Air Force brat, she grew up all over the world before settling in the desert and becoming a cold-weather wimp. Ruth is the author of *You Don't Look Like a Librarian: Shattering Stereotypes and Creating Positive Images in the Internet Age.*

What inspired you to enter the profession?

It was actually a combination of my mother and my job at the time. My mother was a librarian, so I grew up in libraries, and they have always been a part of my life; my job at the time put me in charge of a lot of information management. The more I did, the more I grooved on it, so when I started thinking about future possibilities, the path down the street to the library school seemed a natural one to take.

What has been your most significant accomplishment in your career to date?

Probably doing my job so well I was told, 'Every large project should have someone like you on staff!' Because I'm a solo systems librarian I do a wide variety of tasks, so while there isn't one particular thing I can point to (there are several), the goal of doing my job to the best of my ability is the one I try to reach, and being acknowledged for that was pretty darn spiffy.

What career events have mattered most in your life?

Graduation was pretty big, as was going on to my first formal librarian position. The publication of my first article in *Computers in Libraries*, my first big public presentation at the Special Libraries Association, and the publication of my first book all stand out as well.

What learning, people, or events have stood out in your career or education?

This may seem odd, but being solicited for positions with other large projects was a real eye-opener for me. I've long believed that librarians can do anything, and every librarian I meet reinforces that, but I wasn't applying it directly to myself. I love my job, but had been worried that I had specialized myself into a corner; having these other projects court me made me realize that I really can do anything, and my future possibilities are wide open. It was incredibly liberating, and now I carry on about 'thinking outside the library box' to any new or career-changing librarian who will let me.

What did you need to know in order to manage your career that you learned too late?

Practicalities! Graduate school focused a lot on the theory of things, but didn't touch very much on the real-life day-to-day things a working librarian has to do. I started my first job post-library school – setting up a brand-new small research library – with no hands-on preparation for how to actually order the books to fill the shelves, how to best manage a small space, what database or program to use for cataloging, how to physically process a book, even simple things like call number labels. I actually ended up giving an invited talk about a year after starting titled 'What I Didn't Learn in Library School: From Philosophy to Reality' to a class at a library graduate school. I did eventually get a grip on it all, and the library startup was a success, but it also definitely flavored my first years in the profession.

What are you still interested in learning in terms of managing your career?

I'm fascinated by how different groups of people look for information in an ordered system and how they arrive at different solutions each time. I'd like to continue learning about information architecture, search techniques, database development, and design interfaces so I can address these differences, as well as some more directly applicable things like getting a really good grip on the next iteration of our content management system (Drupal).

Who were/are the two or three top inspirational people for you and why?

(Not including my mother?) Dr. Charles Seavey, my advisor and mentor in graduate school, was amazingly supportive and encouraging to me; it's entirely due to him that I survived the various philosophy of librarianship classes and actually finished school. Liz Bryson of the Canada-France-Hawaii Telescope Corporation and Kathleen Robertson of the Institute for Astronomy (both in Hawaii) were tremendous and calming influences as I was getting my feet under me; they showed me that a solo librarian for an observatory could do it all – provide books and journals, manage electronic document delivery, manage websites – and still have room for creativity and staff interactions. And Stephen Abram has been a great advisor and friend as I moved into the world of conference talks, publications, and leadership roles in a national association.

If you had it to do over again, what would you do differently?

I would have liked to have found this career path a few years earlier than I did. I enjoy what I do so much, and while it's likely I would have had the same set of tasks at my workplace, I wonder what different path I could have taken if I knew more about the profession and what I'd need to do to succeed earlier. I started my first professional job ten days after graduation, and I've already addressed what I didn't know how to do; I'm sure things would have been different if I'd known!

If you had it to do over again, what would you do the same?

I would definitely still have focused on the technical branches of librarianship; I love helping people find the information they're seeking, but I also love the heavy work I do with computer systems, databases, and electronic document systems.

What advice do you have for people entering the profession or people who will be making a significant change in their careers?

Try really hard to think outside the box of traditional librarianship. Be proud that you are a librarian, but be open to jobs that don't necessarily say that in the title, and be open to jobs that are not located in a library. The opportunities are endless!

Speaking at a graduation, what one piece of career advice would you give?

As you head out into libraryland, always be loud and proud that you are a librarian, no matter where you work or what your job title is!

Jane Kinney Meyers

Jane Kinney Meyers is a professional librarian with over 30 years' experience working and living in Africa, consulting, teaching, and working with scores of libraries throughout the continent and participating in the formulation of national information policies of Malawi and Zambia. She lived in Malawi for nearly four years, developing a network of research libraries for the country's Ministry of Agriculture on a World Bank project and pioneering CD-ROM applications for Africa in the mid-1980s. Ten years later she returned to neighboring

Zambia and became increasingly involved with services to street children offered by the Fountain of Hope, a drop-in shelter in Lusaka. She established a reading program, served on the Board, raised funds, and created a library for the children, among her many contributions to the center. After living and working in Zambia from 1998 to 2001, Jane returned to the United States and developed the concept, approach, and organization of the Lubuto Library Project. Honorary lifetime membership in the Zambia Library Association awarded to her in 2006 was joined by wide acclaim in the library profession, including being honored as the 2008 Distinguished Alumnus of the Year by the University of Maryland's College of Information Studies and receiving the 2009 ALA President's Citation for International Innovation.

What inspired you to enter the profession?

The original inspiration came as I was growing up, learning that my mother had gotten a scholarship for both college and medical school at the recommendation of a librarian at the Philadelphia Free Library, who had been approached by a woman physician (in the mid-1930s) who was at the end of her career and wanted to give another woman the same opportunities she had had. My mother had wanted to become a librarian, but had no money to go to college after she finished high school. In the end, she was happy to have become a physician, but I know that this story and the thought that a public library should present such opportunities had a profound influence on me when I was growing up.

What has been your most significant accomplishment in your career to date?

Without a doubt it has been founding the Lubuto Library Project, building a sustainable international development organization from scratch, and allowing library professionals to 'take charge' of the process of developing library systems in Africa.

235

What career events have mattered most in your life?

Establishing a library at the World Bank in the early 1980s, where I was able to be a bit entrepreneurial in terms of promoting inclusion of libraries in development projects – which resulted in a World Bank project in Malawi that took me to live and work in Africa for almost four years, giving me valuable direct, professional experience in international development.

What learning, people, or events have stood out in your career or education?

My work in Malawi from the mid- to late-1980s was pivotal: I took the first CD-ROM to Africa in 1985, established the first positions for professional librarians in Malawi's civil service, and worked directly in an African government developing a national library network in the agriculture sector. This was invaluable experience. Two particular professional mentors, Sal Costabile and Nancy Wynn, taught me a tremendous amount about management and marketing, respectively. The ability to return to Africa in the late 1990s, this time following my husband on a posting in Zambia, allowed me to once again bring library/information entrepreneurship to play in the African environment and plant the seeds for the Lubuto Library Project.

What are you still interested in learning in terms of managing your career?

Nonprofit management and business planning are important challenges still mostly ahead for me.

Who were/are the two or three top inspirational people for you and why?

My mother, Dr. Mary Kinney, who never shrank from a challenge, valued education and learning tremendously, worked extremely hard, always gave to the community and society, and maintained wisdom and humor throughout. Sal Costabile taught me how to put together a consulting organization that does high quality work and brings out the best in its employees. Nancy Wynn showed me how being a first-rate reference librarian, offering intelligent, proactive and effective services, is essential in marketing library/ information services in an organization.

If you had it to do over again, what would you do differently?

I would try to establish the Lubuto Library Project earlier than I did, because that would have given me more time to get it on a sustainable course and have wider impact before it will be time for me to retire.

If you had it to do over again, what would you do the same?

Made the choice to go off to live and work in Malawi, because that experience opened new worlds for me and charted the course of the rest of my career.

What advice do you have for people entering the profession or people who will be making a significant change in their careers?

Be original, have courage, understand what is fundamental and valuable about our profession, and never waiver in knowing how important it is and trying to help others understand that. Learn from your colleagues.

Speaking at a graduation, what one piece of career advice would you give?

Take risks, do not go into this field for security, understand the power and value of our profession, and take every opportunity to learn. Also, listen to how those outside of our profession understand it and what is important to them.

Alison Miller

Alison Miller is the manager of ipl2 Reference Services for Drexel University. (ipl2 is the result of a merger of the Internet Public Library and the Librarians' Internet Index.) She is currently pursuing her Doctorate of Professional Studies in information management at Syracuse University, School of Information Studies. Alison's research interests include collaboration of faculty and librarians in asynchronous, synchronous, and hybrid environments in distance learning through the lens of social presence theory. She received her MSLIS from the iSchool at Drexel University as a distance student. Alison was named a *Library Journal* Mover & Shaker for Innovation in 2010.

What inspired you to enter the profession?

I entered the library and information science (LIS) profession through a somewhat unusual chain of events. I have a BA in criminology/criminal justice. While working during my studies as a part-time corrections officer in a county jail that housed local and federal inmates, I began to see that many of the inmates were in their late teens, and that more and more of those being committed were young. Included in the duties of my job was library time, an occasion when the inmates were taken to the recreation/church/library room. I first watched as many reluctantly started looking through a small collection of books. I then began donating books and encouraged inmates to check them out. It became apparent that many of them were very much lacking in information literacy skills. At the conclusion of my degree, I stayed on for a while as a corrections officer and began to think about reaching these young inmates before they entered the system – a huge realization for me!

From there I transitioned into a school system as a home–school liaison. Again, at that time I was struck by the lack of information literacy skills. Lucky for me, a youth services coordinator position was posted for the public library in my town. Thus began my career in the library and information field. For six years I worked under an amazing library director who inspired me to obtain my MSLIS.

What has been your most significant accomplishment in your career to date?

My most significant accomplishment to date includes interacting with people in the profession through virtual means. I feel very lucky to be part of a profession that is so collaborative. I work from my home, so my network of colleagues often starts and ends via my laptop. Although I do not leave to go to work in a library or office, I feel I am part of a community.

What career events have mattered most in your life?

One of my most important career events was being introduced to the Internet Public Library through my Master's degree course work. It was such a new experience for me, living and working in a very rural community. I had not had prior interaction with a completely virtual environment. I continued as a volunteer after completing my course work in any way I could. As a result, when a job through Florida State University became available, I applied and was offered the position. I worked virtually as the researcher in distance education for the University for two years and was then offered the manager's position with Drexel University, including the option to continue my virtual employment. I feel my dedication and commitment to the Internet Public Library and LIS in general has played a huge role in where I am in my career today. Additionally, I am enrolled in the Doctorate of Professional Studies Program in Information Management at Syracuse University, School of Information Studies. I am able to continue in practice, while also learning more about research and information management. I am very lucky to learn from and work with many respected individuals in the LIS field. Finally, being named a *Library Journal* Mover & Shaker in 2010 for Innovation was a big accomplishment for me in many ways.

What learning, people, or events have stood out in your career or education?

Distance learning has been a key factor for my education and in my career. When I decided to pursue my MSLIS, I was working at a public library and had two young children. The two schools with LIS programs nearest me were approximately two hours away – it just was not an option to go there. I began researching distance programs and completed my Master's through the distance education program at Drexel University.

Combinations of people and events have stood out. I have been very lucky in meeting and connecting with some amazing people in the library world – including Jill Hurst-Wahl, Dave Lankes, and Lori Bell. These professionals have been so inspirational and supportive that they make me want to be a better LIS professional every day. They and others also encourage me in my goal of giving back to the profession.

What did you need to know in order to manage your career that you learned too late?

It's never too late to learn different ways to manage your career.

What are you still interested in learning in terms of managing your career?

I am very interested in learning research methods in order to study and further contribute to LIS education. I'm interested in learning the various effects of virtual environments and how things will unfold in LIS and other areas of higher education, along with the role of the library and librarians in this continuously changing environment.

Who were/are the two or three top inspirational people for you and why?

Mary Geo Tomion, library director at the public library where I worked as a youth services coordinator, got her MLS in 1976, worked at the university library, and went on to be a school librarian for many years. After retiring from the school, she became director of the Dundee Library. Mary Geo knew everything – she was intelligent and compassionate, and genuinely cared about the patrons. She was extremely involved with the community and loved by everyone. A patron could ask for a book, and Mary Geo would know the exact call number and location. She inspired me to get my MSLIS.

Jill Hurst-Wahl was a presenter at an Upstate New York Special Libraries Association conference – my first professional conference. We talked a bit at the conference and continued our conversation into the virtual environment. She introduced me to the T is for Training group, which I am very grateful for. One of the most amazing things about Jill is her generosity in connecting and promoting other people. She has shared so many valued insights and has connected me to various opportunities through networking. Now, studying for a Doctorate of Professional Studies (DPS) at Syracuse, I am lucky to see Jill in person and she continues to support and enable me to advance in my studies and profession.

Dave Lankes is an amazingly talented and supportive person and a real contributor to the LIS field. I met Dave briefly at an Association for Library and Information Science Education conference and of course was in awe. A few weeks later, I took a chance and sent him an email, calling it fan mail, and asking if there were any projects I might be able to help with. He invited me to be part of the Conversants Project (through which Jill and I also worked together). At the conclusion of the project, Dave made it possible for me to attend my first American Library Association conference to attend the culmination of the project. Our relationship continued, and he has been incredibly supportive of me. Through Syracuse University, Dave is my DPS advisor and a trusted confidant.

If you had it to do over again, what would you do differently? If you had it to do over again, what would you do the same?
I actually am very satisfied with how things have progressed. I feel that each step forward is the result of growth on my part, and I continue to strive to grow. Perhaps one thing that I might have done differently is to pursue a traditional PhD. The in-depth study is very appealing to me.

What advice do you have for people entering the profession or people who will be making a significant change in their careers?
Volunteer! I have learned so much through volunteer work. I would tell the graduates that if they haven't yet done so, volunteer with an organization or project. Volunteering is such an enriching experience and is a wonderful chance to shape and give back to the profession.

Pauline Nicholas

Pauline Nicholas is the electronic reference librarian at the University of the West Indies (UWI), Mona Campus. Prior to accepting the position at the UWI, she served as special librarian and records manager in a number of government and non-government organizations. Pauline is a graduate of UWI and holds a MA degree as well as a BEd degree in LIS. She also holds a Teachers' Diploma from Mico Teachers College, also in Jamaica. In her young career in librarianship, she has already received the 2008 Fulbright Visiting Researcher Scholar Fellowship and the IFLA/OCLC Early Career Fellowship in 2007. She served in various capacities in the Library and Information Association of Jamaica since 2004 and in 2010 was the first vice president. Her goal is to make a significant difference among information professionals in the Caribbean.

What inspired you to enter the profession?

I entered the profession by what I call providence. I entered teacher's college to study geography and social studies. I found myself disliking one of these courses and hence I sought to find a different programme. Only one programme was available at the time – library science. I approached the first few classes with apprehension and uncertainty but I had no choice. My tutor then was a great motivator. She was always sharing inspirational experiences about librarianship that caused me to love it. Today I would exchange this career for nothing. I love to see the information needs of students, staff, and other library patrons satisfied, and I always seek to teach information skills when I interact with patrons.

What has been your most significant accomplishment in your career to date?

In the five years I have been in the profession, I have received two prestigious awards or scholarships because of my contribution to the field in Jamaica.

What career events have mattered most in your life?

I have always wanted to become an academic librarian. And although I spent my initial years in special librarians, years that I enjoyed and learned a lot from, it was when I became employed at UWI that my job experience became more fulfilling.

What learning, people, or events have stood out in your career or education?

I have done training in digital reference service and online learning. These are two areas that I have great interest in as a teacher and a librarian. Digital reference service is my envisioned career path and the area in which I intend to make a difference in Jamaica. This training will always be a part of me.

I have come across some very special people – true librarians, always willing to share information and be a part of my professional development. Prof. Margaret Rouse-Jones is a past university librarian of UWI and she has truly inspired me. Nancy Lensenmayer from the Online Computer Library Centre was another, and she continues to ensure that I grow professionally. In Jamaica there is Mrs Barbara Gordon, a past lecturer at the Department of Library and Information Studies.

What advice do you have for people entering the profession or people who will be making a significant change in their careers?

I would say to those entering the profession: always ask 'what difference can I make? How can I improve the system?'

What advice are you seeking from those who have been in the information profession for a number of years?

I would welcome professional guidance on how to be a successful academic librarian.

Speaking at a graduation, what one piece of career advice would you give?

Choose a career based on your interest and make sure it is something you love; then put everything into it.

Karolien Selhorst

Karolien Selhorst holds a Master's degree in translation (English–Spanish) and a MILS (University of Antwerp) and currently works as digital library manager/knowledge manager in the public library of Vlissingen (Holland). As an independent consultant Karolien advises organizations on knowledge management, change management, and Web 2.0 tools, and provides trainings for information professionals and librarians. She is chief editor of her own magazine *Digitale Bibliotheek*, a digital library magazine in the Netherlands. In 2009 Karolien became standing committee member of IFLA's Knowledge Management Section.

What inspired you to enter the profession?

I was fascinated by the mission of libraries: they enrich people's lives and help develop people's information skills to participate in an active way in society. Libraries add value to people's lives in many ways.

What has been your most significant accomplishment in your career to date?

I have assisted others to share knowledge and experience and to work together, and I have shown many people the possibilities of social media and how to use them for adding quality to their lives.

What career events have mattered most in your life?

The decision to start my own magazine in the Netherlands.

What learning, people, or events have stood out in your career or education?

One person who stands out in my career is my current employer, Kees Hamann. He has always believed strongly in me and has given me many opportunities to position myself in the library field.

What did you need to know in order to manage your career that you learned too late?

It's never too late to learn, I believe. What matters at all times is that you respect the people you manage.

What are you still interested in learning in terms of managing your career?

I want to broaden my information and communication technology skills and my human resource skills (competency management, for instance).

Who were/are the two or three top inspirational people for you and why?

My current employer, Kees Hamann, is the person who inspired me most. He has a clear vision where libraries are heading in the future. A vision which most of the time is not very popular with fellow librarians – however, he has often been proved right. I have learned a lot from him when it comes to managing people.

If you had it to do over again, what would you do differently?

I would not do anything differently.

If you had it to do over again, what would you do the same?

I feel I have taken the right decisions at the right time and have met the right people at the right time.

What advice do you have for people entering the profession or people who will be making a significant change in their careers? Speaking at a graduation, what one piece of career advice would you give?

Do not become a librarian because you love books, but because you love people!

Bente Lund Weisbjerg

Bente Weisbjerg is community outreach librarian and immigrant integration project offer for the public libraries in several cities in Denmark. Her focus is project work intended to support integration of ethnic minority immigrants by offering library services tailored to the specific needs of newcomers from a wide variety of cultures. Along with a team of colleagues, she recently completed a 'bridge building' project in which 12 interns received instruction for a year in library work to prepare them for permanent positions at the public library or in the private sector. Her current project is a high-profile, women-only, 'we read the newspaper – together' series of discussion groups in which immigrant woman learn about the society and culture of Denmark, gain confidence to support their families as they navigate through life, and build their personal resources.

What inspired you to enter the profession?
My experience as an au pair in London – taking in all the cultures and languages in that true melting pot city – is no doubt at the root of the fact that I'm now working with immigrants. However, the impetus for library school was the poor compensation from working as a maid at a resort near Copenhagen!

What has been your most significant accomplishment in your career to date?
Establishing the learning center in an immigrant 'ghetto' where 99 languages are spoken was a major achievement. The learning center supplies help and materials for students and job seekers in areas such as computer skills and language training. Prior to determining what the center was going to do and how, I needed to perform detailed research in the community, and that experience – speaking to everyone from

the police officers to the clergy – taught me a great deal about how libraries can support new citizens as they adjust to school, professional education, work, and community life.

What career events have mattered most in your life?

Getting into project work has been a major eye opener for me. It has allowed me to use skills I wasn't sure I had and develop other skills more. It is incredibly rewarding to launch something new and participate in all the stages from concept to operationalization.

What learning, people, or events have stood out in your career or education?

The outstanding thing for me is experiencing how the library clients are the ones to define what the library does. As an outreach 'streetwalker' I never knew what each new day would bring in terms of the challenges brought to me. Imagine a group event where 20 languages and five interpreters are at it simultaneously! Imagine witnessing a woman experiencing for the very first time in her life that anyone is asking her opinion about a story in the news!

What did you need to know in order to manage your career that you learned too late?

Quite soon in my career as a librarian I got a job in the outreach unit, and I will celebrate 25 years there. In the last several years it has become apparent right away that I am suited very well for project oriented work and truly thrive on it – so that's how I will continue.

What are you still interested in learning in terms of managing your career?

I will never stop being eager to conceive, plan, and implement new projects to support the community, and I will gain any new skill I need on the fly.

Who were/are the two or three top inspirational people for you and why?

I have been inspired by my big family – we were nine children. Later on by gifted mentor Niels Holstein-Rathlou as I became a project leader, and lately by a lecturer from the Danish Royal School of Library and Information Science, Hans Elbeshausen. These two 'rearranged my brain' and taught me how to think creatively and be practical at the same time, how to incorporate implementation and evaluation into project planning as soon as an idea hits, and to focus on relevance and value for the target groups. Many years ago, in a single eye-opening lecture, Ulla de Stricker showed me how networking and PR are top priority daily tasks for *all* members of an organization.

If you had it to do over again, what would you do differently?

I wouldn't change a thing except maybe skip that resort maid job!

If you had it to do over again, what would you do the same?

Getting involved in project management has been the best thing ever for me.

What advice do you have for people entering the profession or people who will be making a significant change in their careers?

My advice is for new librarians to look for opportunities to use the professional credentials in settings that appeal to them in other ways, combining innate interests with work. In other words, what gives you satisfaction and pride in general is a big hint about where you might be happy in your career.

Speaking at a graduation, what one piece of career advice would you give?
Go for it even if you've never done anything like it before!

Questions our colleagues want to ask

We asked our colleagues what questions they would want to ask of leaders in the information industry. We offer their responses below as examples of questions you may want to ask your colleagues and mentors:

> When will public library funding be adequate for all the wonderful things we could do and achieve?
>
> Is the future of libraries digital or will the physical library remain?
>
> What makes a good librarian?
>
> I always want to improve – would you be willing to provide feedback?
>
> What is the best way to accelerate change in the profession?
>
> How do you stay on top of things in this crazy, fast-changing profession?
>
> What did you do to stay on top of developments? What did you do to stay 'Information Queen' or 'Information King'?
>
> What I want to know from information industry leaders is how to open the dialogue with professionals and customers about the problems that need to be solved for organizational success. Once the problems are defined, the opportunities flow. How do you offer

information based solutions in innovative ways to convince organizations to seize the success an information professional can offer?

What do you think will happen next in the profession and in the information industry?

How does one stay informed and relevant? How does one become and stay a leader in the information industry?

How do I grow a new organization with a highly skilled and motivated staff? How do you balance your job, your home life, and higher involvement in a professional association, without losing your sanity?

How do you keep the passion? So many professionals worldwide burn out and look for career changes or move from one organization to another. How did you keep the passion alive long enough to make this your life's career?

What can I do to get a proper full time job right now? In all seriousness, that is what I would want to ask. I graduated right into the Great Recession and all I have been able to find so far is short-term contract work.

How do you have time to do it all?

15

Jill and Ulla speak:
our professional journeys

We are not done with our careers – by a long shot – but we are able to look back on invaluable experience we are eager to share with those entering an information profession now *and* with those who have been our colleagues for some time.

Our common theme is twofold: we were blessed to have opportunities to do work uniquely suited to our individual professional approaches and personal characteristics; and no matter what challenges we encountered, we looked for and received the input we needed to deal constructively with them and move on, the stronger and wiser for the experience.

Jill's story

Growing up, I thought I would be like my one grandfather who had worked most of his life as a linotypist-machinist for a newspaper. He loved his work and the people he worked with, and retired when the time was right. I don't think he ever agonized over his job or wondered if his job was secure. That was the life I wanted, but that's not the life I got!

In fifth grade, I began working in a library and worked in libraries throughout my school years and into college. I enjoyed being around the books and understanding what information was in them. A library held everything I needed to know, or so I thought. After college I worked in radio for a couple of years, then went to graduate school for my MLS degree. There I learned about microcomputers, which led to my first professional position, not in a library but in a data center providing end-user support. After five years in IT I became the supervisor of a corporate business library doing competitive intelligence research. Later I moved to a different corporation, working in competitive intelligence and helping to develop a new search engine. In 1998 I decided that being my own boss was the thing to do and started Hurst Associates, Ltd. Now I'm not only consulting but also full-time faculty in Syracuse University's School of Information Studies.

My goal of working for the same organization flew out the window when I was in my 30s. Looking back on my career, I know I have always liked new challenges and opportunities. Thus, doing the same job for 40 years is not something I could have done. Thankfully, I've built the skills and capabilities that have allowed me to move, grow, and never be bored.

Definitely not a straight line

You can see that my career has not progressed in a straight line. In fact, you might realize I have had several careers. The US Department of Labor has said that people change careers about seven times in a lifetime, and that doesn't take into account the number of jobs one person might have during each career. I'm now on my fifth career. My first one – working in radio – was fun, though it paid very little. I worked behind the scenes scheduling programs and commercials as well as making announcements. Although I worked in radio for only four years, that experience has continued to impact my life. From it, I became a more confident public speaker and learned how to speak 'off the cuff'. It was also the first job in which I interacted with people, for example advertisers, in different parts of the country. I was part of something bigger than just the organization I worked in.

There were two additional important takeaways from my radio days. First, since I didn't get paid big bucks, I had to learn how to budget my money. I made dollars and pennies stretch and still found ways to save money for my future. A key component was understanding what I was spending money on and why. If you haven't paid attention to what you are spending money on, you might want to track it for several months. I can guarantee that it will be educational and perhaps life changing. Second, I began to see how information flowed from an event and through the media. Later in graduate school, I was exposed to how information flowed through print sources. This progression – known as the information life cycle – has continued to be important to me and I believe that seeing it from the viewpoint of the news media has given me an advantage.

My five years in IT allowed me to understand how corporate data centers operate and how IT interacts with users. The knowledge I gained about how hardware works and software functions has continued to serve me well. I also learned the pressures IT professionals are under, which has made me a more sympathetic user.

Of course, my goal had always been to be a librarian and my dream came true in 1989. Late in 1988, two people stopped in my office to ask directions so they could get to their meeting. As they left, one person asked, 'Do you have an MLS?' That encounter led to my first professional job as a librarian. I became the supervisor of a new corporate library and had the responsibility of hiring staff, developing services, acquiring resources, and growing the client base.

My career has been a series of events that could be described as being in the right place at the right time. Nearly every career move I have made has contained that element, including my move to becoming a consultant. Although that move is not one I ever anticipated, I was in the right place – mentally, emotionally, and physically – when I made the decision. I had connections to people who were willing to introduce me to potential clients. I also had connections – other consultants – I could watch and learn from. They were not mentors but people who were willing to lift the veil on some of their activities so I could understand how things operated behind the scenes.

I had been teaching in some manner since graduate school, so the move to academia may have been part of a logical progression. I was available when Syracuse University was looking for another adjunct professor, and I had the required knowledge base. Since then, I've been a visiting instructor and an adjunct, and I am now part of the full-time faculty as a professor of practice. Rather than bringing research and theory, I bring real-world experience into the classroom.

Keys to my success

As I look back over my career, I see how four key traits have allowed me to succeed:

A love of learning – I'm always learning and then trying to use what I have learned. It doesn't matter if the knowledge seems unrelated to my area of interest, because I know that at some point it will be helpful. Although this may seems unfocused to you, it has worked for me because I have learned to see how topics relate to each other and how knowledge in one area can be used elsewhere. I know that if

I continue to learn, then my knowledge and skills are continually improving and I'm not becoming stale. Of course, learning by itself is not important – using knowledge is. Using the knowledge I have gained has helped me move in different directions throughout my career.

An attitude of service – Every culture contains the idea that we should 'do for others'. For me, the movie *Pay It Forward* (2000) and the book *29 Gifts* (2009) demonstrate that idea. It's not 'what's in it for me', but 'what's in it for you'. Such an attitude is likely very familiar to you because the desire to serve draws many people to librarianship and the information professions. However, along with doing for others, there is the need to do for yourself. I can't help you if I'm not in a position – professionally, physically, mentally, or emotionally – to be of service. Therefore, I must also take care of myself.

The ability to make connections – This quality I believe I inherited from some of my ancestors. It is the ability to reach out and make a meaningful connection with others as well as the ability to then connect them to potentially useful ideas, services, and other people. Long after my maternal grandmother had died, I remember hearing the story of how she first introduced herself to a new neighbor. As she worked in the garden, my grandmother cut through a vacant field – with garden tools still in hand – so they could meet. I imagine it was not just 'hi, how are you?' but rather a conversation about the neighborhood and its inhabitants. While talking to complete strangers at bus stops, grocery stores, and conferences is something I'm prone to do, I consciously look for opportunities to turn every conversation into a meaningful connection for myself or for someone else. The net effect is that I have created a large extended network.

Standing on powerful shoulders – Sir Isaac Newton said, 'If I have seen further it is only by standing on the shoulders of giants.' In my life, those 'giants' have been friends, colleagues, and people I've met in passing. Many people have taught me important lessons big and small. Lots of people have pushed and pulled me in new directions. And some people have handed me 'balls' and told me to run with them. John Donne said 'no man is an island' and in my life I know that has been true.

Once you have finished reading this book, I hope you will feel confident you can implement those four keys in your life.

Getting my first professional interview

We often repeat the adage that it is not *what* you know, but *who* you know, and this was definitely the case when I got my first professional interview.

In December 1982 I returned to Elmira, NY, to celebrate the Christmas holiday and attend my cousin's funeral. After the funeral, many people went to an aunt's house, and there I talked to a friend of the family who was helping to teach area children about computers. He thought I ought to return to Elmira to work and we made an appointment to get together to talk about what he was doing. A few days later, we met in a cold computer lab (remember it was during the holidays) where he talked about his team's plans and I talked about the computer support work I had been doing as a graduate assistant. I gave him my resume in hopes he would be able to hire me at some point in the future.

A couple of months later, I received a phone call from Corning Glass Works. The caller said I had sent my resume and wondered if I was still interested in a position. But I hadn't sent my resume! Still, I said *yes* I would be interested in whatever opening was available. Corning arranged to fly me from College Park, MD, to Corning, NY, for a day of interviews. The net result was a job offer that I gladly accepted. How had they received my resume? The person I huddled with in Elmira over the Christmas holiday had given my resume to a partner who worked in human resources at Corning, and the partner kept an eye on job openings. When he saw an appropriate opening, the rest – as they say – is history.

Two men were key in putting my resume in the right hands; *what I knew* helped me get the job offer. The lesson for me was that *what I know* is very important, but *who I know* is as important. I've always worked to have a strong network and over the years that network has helped me to find opportunities I never would have found on my own, like that first job at Corning Glass Works.

Acknowledgements

To all others who have offered words of support, criticism, and direction – especially Tom – thank you! You helped to get me where I am today.

Jill's official bio

Jill Hurst-Wahl is Assistant Professor of Practice in Syracuse University's School of Information Studies (iSchool) and President of Hurst Associates, Ltd. Her areas of focus include digitization, digital libraries, copyright, social media, and Web 2.0.

A member of the iSchool since 2001, Jill became full-time faculty in 2009. As part of the interdisciplinary iSchool, she teaches campus and online graduate courses related to library and information science and information management, including 'Creating, Managing & Preserving Digital Assets', 'Digital Libraries', 'Planning, Marketing & Assessing Library Services', and 'Business Resources and Strategic Intelligence'.

As a consultant since 1998, Jill works with organizations that want to become more visible by digitizing materials or implementing social media. She has worked with a variety of cultural heritage organizations on planning and implementing digitization programs and assessing their efforts. Jill advises organizations on how to use social media to promote their activities, including their digital collections.

Before 1998 Jill worked for Corning Incorporated (formerly known as Corning Glass Works) in Corning, NY, and for Manning & Napier Advisors Inc. in Rochester, NY. At those companies she used her knowledge of information technology and information retrieval to create new internal and external services.

Jill is a frequent speaker and author. She has spoken at workshops and conferences in North America and Europe on digitization and social media. As an author, she writes for her own blogs ('eNetworking 101' and 'Digitization 101') as well as for a number of industry publications. Her blogs are highly regarded, 'Digitization 101' being quoted and referenced by people around the world.

Jill belongs to a number of organizations, including the Special Libraries Association (SLA). She has volunteered with SLA at the chapter, division, and association level including chairing the Second Life Work Group (2008) and served as a member of the Information Outlook Advisory Council (2009–2010). In 2010, Jill was elected to the SLA Board of Directors to serve a three year term (2011–2013). She is a member of the New York State Regents Advisory Council on Libraries (2007–2012) and the University of the State of New York's Technology Policy and Practices Council (2009–2014). Jill is also a member of the Franklin W. Olin College of Engineering External IT Advisory Board (2010–2012).

Jill has received several awards including a 2008 SLA Presidential Citation from Stephen Abram 'for leading the development of the SLA's Second Life presence and programs.

Jill's dedication to innovation, and her patience with a largely inexperienced membership, has helped to find a new "place" for future initiatives that is fuzzy, fun, and functional.' In 2007 she was honored as the Minority Small Business Champion by the Syracuse office of the US Small Business Administration covering 34 counties in Upstate New York. The South Central Research Library Council honored her in 1993 with the Distinguished Achievement Award for her work with corporate librarians in the Southern Tier of New York.

Jill received her MLS degree from the University of Maryland. She graduated cum laude with a BA degree from Elmira College, majoring in philosophy/religion and English.

Ulla's story

Looking back over my working life, it is now obvious to me that I 'had to' become a consultant: I am fiercely independent and enterprising by nature. Of course, it's rare for anyone to go straight into consulting from graduate school... a certain amount of professional experience must be accumulated to establish the required credibility and reputation. So I prepared – unwittingly – by working in jobs involving significant leeway to exercise my judgment, and I manifested my innate entrepreneurship in a variety of extracurricular activities such as teaching. The theme of my professional life is entirely in sync with who I am as a person: a freedom loving soul who thrills at making a difference for others.

Why library science?

Many readers may recognize the – in retrospect headshake-inducing – situation in which we apply ourselves with tremendous zeal to studies lacking career prospects. Driven by personal interests, my studies were of a literary nature, and no one in my immediate circles ever subjected me to the 'and how were you proposing to pay the bills?' drill. I wised up sufficiently in the autumn prior to next summer's graduation to realize I absolutely positively had to 'do something practical' and quickly zeroed in on a logical choice: my Master's thesis and my part-time work as a research assistant verifying the accuracy of footnotes in a scholarly biography work had me spending lots of time in McGill University's McLennan Library, and I was aware the Graduate School of Library Science – as it was named at the time – occupied its lower level. Nursing was attractive too, but not having an undergraduate science background, I removed that choice from realistic consideration.

When I confidently marched into the first day of classes at library school, I expected to enter a world of books. Imagine my surprise when I was set up for subsequent events with profound consequences: 'Welcome to Computing 101' almost had me faint – I did not remember signing up for any computer courses! But calm prevailed... and in fact Professor David Batty was a superbly interesting lecturer, explaining the nitty gritty of how libraries were adopting computerized catalogues. I decided to stick it out, opened my mind, and discovered it was prewired to grasp how computers work with text and symbols.

The School's new director, Vivian Sessions, did three life-changing things for me: first, she brought from Lockheed Missiles & Space Corporation one Roger Summit, DIALOG's inventor, to speak to our class. Second, she introduced DIALOG as a teaching tool. You know the old saying about taking to something like a duck does to water? It was as if I had known the DIALOG command syntax all my life. Listening to Roger, I thought, 'My, it would be interesting to work for that company one day.' (In light of the fact that

DIALOG had no representation in Canada, I dismissed the thought.) Third, she created the position of assistant to the director.

My first job, academic: administration

In this role, I had the incredible privilege to support the director by developing teaching schedules, serving on a number of interfaculty committees, assisting in the process of American Library Association accreditation for the School, teaching information retrieval, and serving as an ombudsman for the students. Those efforts allowed me to observe the complex workings of committees and the confusing fact that various interests sometimes are at odds with what *to me* was obviously the logical or most straightforward approach. What ought in my freshly minted professional mind to be quite simple and factual became infused with more nuance. Looking back now, it's all well understood, but at the time I was new to organizational politics.

My second job, commercial: customer service and training

Word came that Lockheed was opening a Canadian office in Toronto at a company called Micromedia Limited. Chalk it up to youth and inexperience... I called the manager of that office and told him, 'You can't do this without me!' On interview, he and Micromedia's owner bought that argument, and I made Toronto my home. I cannot thank Frank Gagne enough for the role he played in building my skills as a young professional. He was unfailingly available to discuss the best approach for any matter that didn't have a clear solution; he fostered a spirit of 'do what is right'; and he had an optimistic and upbeat attitude, which got me through quite a few situations when I wasn't sure I had what it took. Because I could rely on him as a personal supporter as well as a boss, he helped me build a professional confidence I have since tried to build for others.

New in Canada, the Toronto DIALOG office needed to establish a new market. My role as trainer and customer service representative gave me plenty of opportunities to learn what customers need and appreciate – and without a second thought I pulled out all the stops to help 'my' Canadian customers. (I later confessed to my Lockheed masters in Palo Alto, CA, that I proceeded as I believed was best and asked for forgiveness later. It seems what I did was good for sales.) My proudest moment for that role must be when I heard second hand that it was mentioned in public how another company's customer service was 'almost as good as Ulla's'. Thinking back, the key was caring enough about a caller's question to act as an extended public library if the question could not be solved through DIALOG: 'For that question, the [nation's] Embassy may be your best bet' or 'Let me contact someone I know who might have a lead'. On many days in this job, I thought, 'I can't believe they are paying me to enjoy every day!', and on other days I thought, 'I'm not going to survive teaching a full day class with a raging flu and no voice', but in retrospect, it was one fantastic job.

I felt authentic because I was in tune with the work. Developing and teaching seminars and solving customer questions suited me perfectly. I could sink my teeth into every task and work to my own perfectionist standards! Then came promotion to management, and with it an entirely new territory of challenges. Talk about a learning curve... it is one thing to bone up on chemistry to get ready to teach the seminar on how to search the science databases, quite another to figure out how best to help a distraught staff member!

My third, fourth, and fifth jobs: managing and developing

Over time at Micromedia I was given responsibility for several departments and asked to develop a new one. In addition to DIALOG, I looked after a for-fee business information unit and a unit selling corporate documents, and I set up and operated a unit distributing CD-ROM products to Canadian libraries. By and by, I came to occupy a spokesperson role for the company when journalists wanted to know what this 'online thing' was all about.

To start, I read books about how to be a good boss and tried to emulate the principles... but failed miserably! To this day I thank a brave staff member who said to me 'we miss the real Ulla'. As in 'the authentic, immediate, personal, genuine Ulla who uses her intuition and good sense rather than rules from a book'. No amount of money could have paid for the realization that being your true self is paramount, and I use every opportunity to tell the story when I speak about career matters.

Such revelations were plentiful as I matured through those years. They covered 'duh' discoveries – while I thought nothing of a three-week business trip, those with families understandably object to being away for that long – and humbling ones such as being thrust into the role of managing staff whose day to day activities I did not know in detail. I found out that 'being there' for my staff meant just that – dropping everything else when someone needed my advice or a team needed to handle unforeseen circumstances. Dealing with the inevitable differences of opinion took a great deal of tact and finesse, not to mention time. Hiring a new staff member, I soon realized, is not for the faint of heart – much as I looked for the spark of engagement more than I cared about formal qualifications, it's difficult to predict a good fit with the team from a brief interview. But perhaps the most exciting lesson I took with me is this one: encouraging a staff member to step out of comfort zones and watching him or her grow in the job is among the privileges of being in charge. I love the memory of gently nudging someone unconvinced of being ready for a given task, creating opportunities for practicing or coaching, and then watching proudly as he or she taught that first seminar or put together that first workbook.

In taking on the building and launching of the CD-ROM Centre (it sounds so quaint now!), I demonstrated to myself it is possible to do something completely new and make it up as you go. With the fantastic support from business professionals in other departments and from my small team, I 'just did it' according to the principle of putting myself in customers' shoes.

In the course of my tenure at Micromedia, I was delighted and exhilarated... and miserable when the workload overwhelmed me or a personnel matter had me totally stumped and the rest of the team members were affected. There was lots of voluntary overtime work; Monday mornings were less harried if I had spent a Saturday or Sunday (often both) catching up on desk work. Yes, I worked like a dog – how could I not? But the overriding quality of those years was a sense I had something meaningful to offer to customers and to my staff. I loved the work because I felt (and was told) I made a difference.

My last job before moving into consulting

Out of the blue came the question 'would you like to head up the new electronic publishing unit we are building?' Carswell, a Canadian legal publishing unit of Thomson, was about to develop a case law database and needed someone with insight into online searching. What with the industry having matured and my feeling that I had brought my departments at Micromedia to a healthy, sustainable state... the opportunity was just too good to pass up. My marching orders were to oversee the conversion of over two hundred years of legal decisions from print to electronic form and to develop an intuitive menu-driven search interface to go with it – well before something called the internet emerged! On system launch, I was to orchestrate the in-person introduction of the new system to Canada's top law firms.

I embarked on the challenging project, learning fast about the world of technical product development, alpha and beta testing, and the vagaries of using data from tapes *predating* proofread and knife-corrected master print plates. I learned about the market impact of customer trust in a publisher and in tried-and-true sources, and I discovered the influence of opinion leaders and about the need to develop relationships with them.

Naturally, customer service was essential so I set up and managed a small team using the principles that had worked so well at Micromedia. Serving lawyers as well as librarians added a twist, but the basic principle remained: the customer needs us to do whatever it takes to help him or her – *now*.

Tax legislation followed case law. Time flew by as I undertook more development and market introduction projects at Carswell.

And then I set up shop!

For some years, I'd been hearing 'you ought to set out on your own' and countering 'ah, but you have an income producing spouse'. Yet there came a day when I was ready.

I proposed a phasing-out arrangement so the current projects would be finished over the next year, and it was readily accepted. Thus, I had a small buffer between secure income and... no assurance of income at all!

The very next day, the phone rang. 'We are rolling out a new online product and... do you know anything about customer service?'

One of the themes in our book is developing a personal brand. It soon became clear, once my consulting shingle was out, that all along in my career I had inadvertently done just that – through being in customer facing roles and through being visible in associations, at conferences, and in articles. Today, I ascribe my brand to a natural inclination toward doing my very best to assist others – but in retrospect I encourage everyone to be deliberate about establishing a strong professional profile early on.

In the first years of my work as a consultant, projects tended to have an information industry focus – product strategies and development, client relations, and marketing. Over time, the nature of my projects has evolved as the clients' needs have; at this juncture, I characterize my work as being broadly associated with strategic planning. As expenditure for information and knowledge-related activities receive ever greater scrutiny, and as the perception seems to persist that 'with the internet, we don't need information professionals', my clients turn to me for assistance in aligning and positioning information services. With every project, I encounter outstanding professionals doing amazing work, and from every project I take away insights to add to my experience.

My extracurricular activities

Early on, I joined the Special Libraries Association (SLA) because 'it seemed the place to be' and through the years have served in several roles, president of the Toronto Chapter and chair of the Leadership and Management Division among them. For as long as I can remember, I have offered my colleagues in SLA a free resume review service. To this day, I continue to belong to professional associations, and I am categorical in my opinion that information professionals *must* be active in whatever associations are most appropriate for them. The benefit of connections made through participating actively in professional associations is priceless, and so are the opportunities for learning and growing in a safe environment.

I got busy in other non-work areas too. I pitched to a local college the notion of a program of courses in online searching and had the pleasure of devising courses, teaching, and bringing on board other instructors. In another local college's library technician program, I taught (and enticed a colleague to come along and co-teach) to prepare students for careers in the information and publishing industries.

All along, I have offered and continue to offer to speak at conference or seminar events and to meet with groups of professionals. I'm always keen to write articles, and for faculties of information studies (variously named) I offer career-related lectures to students on request.

You might ask why I took on 'second jobs' doing volunteer projects: was it not enough to do well in the day job? My answer is that we are all different in how we approach our careers, but I could not imagine a life without these extras. I am *that interested* in the profession and in my colleagues' success!

269

Lessons learned

In earlier chapters, there is more detail about the challenges of the workplace. For now, here is a sampling of insights I did not hear about in school.

Politics

- Nothing is quite what it seems. Ask questions and get the full story before leaping to conclusions.

- Some reports need to be revised more than a few times before the text meets the purpose for which it was originally intended. 'The truth' can be described in many ways.

- Among a group, any technical or circumstantial description will be interpreted in as many ways as there are individuals in it. Having explained something does not mean it has been understood or that it will lead to desired behaviors.

Customer relations

- Dependability is a powerful respect builder. If you say 'I'll call you back within the hour' and then do so to report what you have found out so far, the client will almost always accept the message you have even if it isn't exactly what was wanted.

- A sincere and sincerely communicated willingness to do the utmost for the customer outweighs any disappointment he or she may feel at the price, the license terms, the time it will take to produce a report, and so on.

- Going the extra mile and performing a service over and above what is required yields benefits for years to come. Happy customers don't forget.

- Customers talk to each other about the service they receive.

Team building and staff development

- It takes a great deal of attention and effort to be the kind of manager staff members appreciate; every day there are challenges, pitfalls, opportunities to recognize someone for doing a great job, and moments when there are only a few seconds to decide what is the right thing to do.

- A manager's top priority is to foster the kind of environment in which team members look forward to coming to work and in which they are enabled to produce quality results consistently.

- Some staff members are too shy or fearful to come and say 'I have a problem'. A manager must look out – sensitively – for potential difficulties and address them proactively.

Acknowledgements

Collegial support is paramount in any career. I would like to give credit to all those who helped me become a confident professional and to all those who supported me as loyal members of my teams. In the interest of confidentiality, 'you know who you are'.

I thank you all for hiring me and promoting me and giving me ever more diverse business projects; for trusting me to represent your faculty and company; for giving me the latitude to do things my way; for pitching in on weekends and evenings to catch up with workload when I needed you; for taking the time to listen; and for teaching me that 'perception is reality'.

Above all, I thank every one of you who gave me your friendship as we worked together through the years. You have meant more to me than you know.

Ulla's official bio

With experience since the late 1970s in the information industry and information related operations, Ulla focuses in her consulting engagements on strategic planning for an organization's information and knowledge management policies, practices, and delivery mechanisms including specialized libraries. In consulting practice since late 1992, she has built a strong track record executing numerous information audits and needs assessment studies and recommending approaches for dealing with information services and knowledge management challenges. Prior to 1992 she held senior positions in the information industry in customer facing and product development roles.

Ulla is known for her special attention to the impact of corporate culture and extrinsic pressures on the actual day to day practices of knowledge workers, and frequently conducts strategic planning studies based on such practices. Typical projects have focused on assessments of knowledge worker requirements, determination of priorities relating to information support content and services, and structuring of underlying operations to deliver such content and services in effective ways.

Ulla speaks frequently at information management related conferences and contributes frequently to information industry journals. Several seminars and articles are publicly available at *www.destricker.com*, as is her information and knowledge management blog.

She is the author of *Business Cases for Info Pros: Here's Why, Here's How*, Information Today, 2008 (*http://books .infotoday.com/books/BusinessCasesforInfoPros.shtml*) and *Is Consulting for You?*, American Library Association, 2007 (*www.alastore.ala.org/detail.aspx?ID=401*).

Ulla developed and teaches the course 'Information Audit' in the University of Toronto iSchool Institute (formerly the Faculty of Information's Professional Learning Centre). She is active in the SLA (sla.org) and was elected to its board of directors for 2011–2013. In addition, she was a board member of the Association of Independent Information Professionals (aiip.org) from 2008 to 2010. She offers career guidance and resume assistance voluntarily to hundreds of information professionals every year. In 2009 she received AIIP's Sue Rugge Memorial Award for her support to colleagues.

Epilogue

Ulla: thoughts for encouragement

We have shared our experience in hopes it will benefit our current and future colleagues. Now we send each of you on your way in hopes you will create an exciting and rewarding career – one that suits your unique combination of innate abilities, interests, education, and experience so you may feel fulfilled in your work.

As I take my leave – for now – I offer these last thoughts to encourage you:

- Never be afraid of hard work. Think of it as an investment in yourself and your current and future professional achievement and personal contentment.

- Although no one can control external events and conditions, everyone can control how he or she reacts and acts. Choose reactions and actions reflecting your highest standards.

- What goes around, comes around. Believe that going the extra mile will be rewarded – albeit in unexpected ways.

- What you focus on, you get more of. 'Cut off the oxygen' to negativity and 'feed energy' to positive thoughts and efforts.

- See the benefit in every circumstance and situation: from doing this paper or this work, I am learning and growing.

If I approach this meeting with a constructive attitude, I will have an opportunity to derive a positive outcome for everyone. By structuring my group this way, I will enhance the chances for everyone to expand his or her skills.

- Expect success. You deserve it.

Jill: make it so!

In the TV show *Star Trek: The Next Generation*, Captain Jean-Luc Picard asks his crew members to jump into action using the words 'make it so'. You have now completed reading a book of advice about your career and it is time for you to jump into action, plan your future, and make it so.

Undoubtedly, the book has prompted ideas, given you suggestions, and brought to mind actions you might take. Write them down, if you have not done so already, and begin to plan how you are going to implement them. Create action steps that you will start tomorrow, even if the actions seem like small steps. Remember that a journey of a thousand miles starts with one step. So, too, your career is helped by every small step you take.

Keep in mind that you control your future. We often forget that and leave our careers and our futures in the hands of others. Only you have your best interest truly in mind. Even if you hesitate to move forward, recognize it is your job to ensure your future is what you want, including your career. Like the job responsibilities you have at work, you have responsibilities for managing your career from now until the day you retire. And when you retire, you should be able to look back at what you created and be very pleased!

Don't just sit there... make it so!

Resources

At the end of the movie *The Time Machine*, H.G. Wells returns to the future and takes three books with him. Although his friends wonder what books he chose, the real question becomes what books they each would take if they had been in his shoes. If Ulla and Jill had been in H.G. Wells' position, here are the books they would have selected:

Carnegie, Dale. *How To Win Friends and Influence People.* First published in 1937 and republished multiple times since. New York: Simon & Schuster, 2009.

De Bono, Edward. *Six Thinking Hats.* New York: Little, Brown & Co., 1999.

Gelb, Michael J. *How to Think Like Leonardo da Vinci: Seven Steps to Genius Every Day.* New York: Dell Publishing, 1998.

Gerber, Michael. *The E-Myth Revisited: Why Most Small Businesses Don't Work and What to Do About It.* New York: HarperCollins, 1995.

Hicks, Esther, and Jerry Hicks. *Ask and It Is Given.* Carlsbad, CA: Hay House, 2009.

Hill, Napoleon. *Think and Grow Rich.* First published in 1937 and republished multiple times since. New York: Fall River Press, 2010.

Kneale, Ruth. *You Don't Look Like a Librarian: Shattering Stereotypes and Creating Positive New Images in the Internet Age.* Medford, NJ: Information Today, Inc., 2009.

Schwartz, David J. *The Magic of Thinking Big.* New York: Simon & Schuster, 1959.

Index

29 Gifts, 257
Abram, Stephen, 210, 229–30, 233, 260
Advanced Technology Solar Telescope, 230
Air Force (US), 231
Alliance Library System, 106
American Library Association (ALA), 225–6, 242, 263, 272
ALA President's Citation for International Innovation, 235
Arnold, Stephen E., 203
Ask and It Is Given, 277
Association of Independent Information Professionals (AIIP), 273
Sue Rugge Memorial Award, 273

Batty, David, 262
Bell, Lori, 240
Bibliothek 2.0 und mehr, 209
Boston College, 225
Bryson, Liz, 233
Business Cases for Info Pros: Here's Why, Here's How, 272
ByWater Solutions, 215

California Library Association Intellectual Freedom Committee, 214
Canada-France-Hawaii Telescope Corporation, 233
Canada Library Association, 229
Carnegie, Dale, 277
Carswell (a unit of Thomson), 266
Central New York Library Resources Council, 198
CLRC Mentoring Toolkit, 198
CERN, 208–10
Scientific Information Service, 208
Chandos, 215
Computers in Libraries (journal), 231
Confessions of a Mad Librarian, 211
Coon, Kathy, 217
Cormack, Chris, 218
Corning Incorporated, 260
Corning Glass Works, 258–9
Costabile, Sal, 236–7

Danish Royal School of Library and Information Science, 249
De Bono, Edward, 277
de Stricker, Ulla, 203, 220, 229, 249
DIALOG, 262–5
Digitale Bibliotheek, 245

Digitization 101, 260
Dominican University, 206
Donne, John, 258
Drexel University, 216, 238–40
   iSchool, 238
Dundee Library, 241

Elbeshausen, Hans, 249
Elmira College, 261
Elsevier, 225
   Scopus, 225
E-Myth Revisited: Why Most
     Small Businesses Don't Work
     and What to Do About It,
     The, 277
eNetworking 101, 260
European Library Automation
   Group (ELAG), 209
European Organization for
   Nuclear Research, 208

Facebook, 193
Fisher, Bill, 213
Florida State University, 239
Fogle, Lynn, 203
Fountain of Hope, 235
Franklin W. Olin College of
   Engineering External IT
   Advisory Board, 160
Frye Leadership Institute, 222–3
Fulbright Visiting Researcher
   Scholar Fellowship, 243

Gagne, Frank, 263
Gelb, Michael J., 277
Gemini Observatory, 230
   Gemini 8m Telescopes Project,
   230

Gerber, Michael, 277
Google Book Project, 212
Gordon, Barbara, 244

Hamann, Kees, 245–6
Hicks, Esther, 277
Hicks, Jerry, 277
Hill, Napoleon, 277
Holstein-Rathlou, Niels, 249
How to Think Like Leonardo da
     Vinci: Seven Steps to Genius
     Every Day, 277
How to Win Friends and
     Influence People, 277
Humboldt University, 209
Hurst Associates, Ltd., 254
Hurst-Wahl, Jill, 240–2, 259

ibiblio.org, 227
IFLA
   Knowledge Management
     Section, 245
IFLA/OCLC Early Career
   Fellowship, 243
Information Today, 215, 272
Institute for Astronomy, 233
Institute of Science and
   Technology Austria, 208
International Federation of
   Library Associations and
   Institutions (IFLA), 208–9
Internet Librarian Conference,
   216
Internet Librarian International,
   209
Internet Public Library, 239
   ipl2 Reference Services, 238
Is Consulting for You?, 272

Jenkins Law Library, 215–18
Jobs, Steve, 210
Jones, Paul, 227

Kentucky Libraries Association, 202
Kinney, Mary, 236
Kneale, Ruth, 278
Koha Integrated Library System, 218

Lankes, Dave, 240–2
Lensenmayer, Nancy, 244
Librarians' Internet Index, 238
Library and Information
    Association of Jamaica, 243
Library Journal, 215, 238, 240
    Movers & Shakers, 215, 238, 240
Library Mashups, 215
LinkedIn, 193
Livingston, Shawn, 204
Lockheed Missiles & Space
    Corporation, 262, 264
Los Angeles Herald Examiner, 212
Los Angeles (L.A.) Times, 212
Los Angeles Public Library
    (LAPL), 211–12
Luboto Library Project, 235–7
Lux, Claudia, 209–10

Magic of Thinking Big, The, 278
Manning & Napier Advisors Inc., 260
McGill University, 262
    Graduate School of Library
        Science, 262–3
    McLennan Library, 262
Mico Teachers College, 243

Micromedia Limited, 89, 263, 265–7
Ministry of Agriculture (Malawi), 234
Minow, Mary, 213

Netherlands Red Cross, 220
Newton, Isaac, 257
New York State Regents Advisory
    Council on Libraries, 260
*Next Generation Corporate
    Libraries and Information
    Services*, 201

Online Computer Library Centre, 244
Ontario Library Association, 229

PATRIOT Act, 225
Patton, Elaine P., 201
Pay it Forward, 257
Philadelphia Free Library, 235
Picard, Jean-Luc, 276
Pope, Kitty, 207
*Practical Open Source Software
    for Libraries*, 215
ProQuest, 89

Resume resources on the web, 75, 86
Robertson, Kathleen, 233
Rouse-Jones, Margaret, 244

San Jose State University, 206, 213–14
    School of Library and
        Information Studies, 206, 211
Santa Clara University School of
    Law, 211

Schwartz, David J., 278
Seavey, Charles, 233
Second Life, 206, 260
Sessions, Vivian, 262
Six Thinking Hats, 277
Sizemore, Cammie, 204
South Central Regional Library
    Council, 261
  Distinguished Achievement
    Award, 261
Special Libraries Association
    (SLA), 195, 201, 214, 222–4,
    229, 231, 241, 260, 269, 273
  Academic Division, 222
  Board of Directors, 260, 273
  Information Outlook Advisory
    Council, 260
  Information Technology
    Division, 222
  Kentucky Chapter, 201–3
  Kentucky Virtual Library
    Advisory Committee, 201
  Leadership and Management
    Division, 269
  Legal Division, 201, 203
  News Division, 214
  Second Life Work Group, 260
  SLA Presidential Citation, 260
  Toronto Chapter, 269
  Upstate New York Chapter,
    241
Staatsbibliothek zu Berlin, 208
Stanford University, 212
Star Trek, 173
  Enterprise, 173
Star Trek: The Next Generation, 276
Stephens, Michael, 210, 227
Summit, Roger, 262

Syracuse University, 201, 238–9,
    241–2, 254, 256, 259
  School of Information Studies,
    238–9, 254, 259

T is for Training, 241
Tame the Web, 227
Think and Grow Rich, 277
Thomson, 266
  Carswell, 266–7
Time Machine, The, 277
Toastmasters International, 157
Tomion, Mary Geo, 241
Twitter, 193, 220

Uncommon Commons, The, 222
University of Antwerp, 245
University of Illinois, 206
University of Kentucky, 202
  Graduate History Program, 202
  Information Commons
    (The Hub), 222
  Library and Information
    Science Graduate School, 202
University of Kentucky Libraries,
    222
University of Maryland, 261
  College of Information Studies,
    235
University of North Carolina
    (UNC), 225, 227
  School of Information and
    Library Science, 225, 227
University of the State of
    New York Technology Policy
    and Practices Council, 260
University of the West Indies
    (UWI), 242–4

Department of Library and
Information Studies, 244
University of Toronto, 273
Faculty of Information's
Professional Learning Centre,
273
iSchool Institute, 273
US Department of Labor, 254
US Small Business Administration,
261
Minority Small Business
Champion, 261

Vaynerchuk, Gary, 230
Vlissingen public library, 245

Wales, Jimmy, 210
Weinberger, David, 210

Wells, H.G., 277
Western Illinois University, 206–7
What I Learned Today, 215, 217
Wikimedia Germany, 209
Wilford, Valerie, 207
World Bank, 234, 236
Wynn, Nancy, 236–7

*You Don't Look Like a Librarian:
Shattering Stereotypes and
Creating Positive Images in
the Internet Age*, 231, 278
Yu, Cabot, 89

Zambia Library Association,
235
Zentral und Landesbibliothek
Berlin, 208

Breinigsville, PA USA
10 February 2011
255336BV00003B/4/P